MW01233686

TRANSFORMATIONAL
VISION

SEEING THE WORLD
THROUGH THE
EYES OF JESUS

STAN TOLER
& DAN SCHAFER

www.wgm.org

TABLE OF CONTENTS

INTRODUCTION

Over 150,000 people will die today, and 40 percent of those souls will enter eternity with little or no access to the gospel of Jesus Christ. Tomorrow will be the same.

Stan Toler and Dan Schafer have given their lives in seeking to change that statistic. Their mission was and is to help you believe so much in what you can do by the power of the Holy Spirit that you will join them in spirit and in service.

THE AWESOME MOMENT

Transformational Vision comes from the awesome moment when Jesus overlooked the city and grieved over those who lived there without faith in Who He is and what He offered them. Luke 13:34, "Jerusalem, Jerusalem, you who kill the prophets and stone those sent to you, how often I have longed to gather your children together, as a hen gathers her chicks under her wings, and you were not willing."

As He turned the page of His ministry on earth to return to heaven's eternal throne, He put world evangelism and discipleship into human hands. Into your hands and ours. John 20:21, "As the Father has sent me, I am sending you." So He wants you to see the world as He sees you.

THE TASK

He created us, so He knows how very human we are to face a superhuman task. "He is not willing that any should perish, but that all should come to repentance" (2 Peter 3:9). Even as Jesus saw the needs of Jerusalem and the world, He saw the possibilities in you to meet them.

And as He spent His final years on earth teaching, affirming, and loving His disciples, He offers the same preparation to you through His Word, His Holy Spirit, and His anointed teachers. *Transformational Vision* is a book of 30 Bible studies and testimonies of transformation from World Gospel Mission that will refire your missionary passion to reach your world.

THE URGENCY

This is one of the last writing projects of best-selling author, Dr. Stan Toler (1950-2017). He teamed with World Gospel Mission president, Dr. Dan Schafer, to share the urgency of transformational leadership and ministry in a world that has largely abandoned its spiritual roots.

Dr. Schafer, a former missionary himself, leads a team of missionaries who are willing to put their lives on the line to reach souls in every nation with the gospel. Their stories will give you a glimpse of the world in which they served or serve and will challenge you to dream their dreams.

THE PROMISE

As you read *Transformational Vision*, remember that the Savior who sends you to the nearest or farthest regions of the earth promised to go with you.

And when the task seems gigantic or when you feel inadequate, remember that the One who burdens your heart for the lost will give you the lift of His spiritual power to carry out your mission. "You will receive power when the Holy Spirit comes on you; and you will be my witnesses in Jerusalem, and in all Judea and Samaria, and to the ends of the earth" (Acts 1:8).

Stan Toler and Dan Schafer, 2017

1

PERFECTLY CAPABLE

STAN TOLER

*"And this is my prayer: that your love may
abound more and more in knowledge and depth of
insight, so that you may be able to discern what
is best and may be pure and blameless for
the day of Christ."
- Philippians 1:9–10*

God sees you as perfectly capable to reach His
world with the Good News. You're a winner, no
matter the challenges. But improvement is the objective of
every winner. Paul wrote, "We instructed you how to live
in order to please God, as in fact you are living. Now we
ask you and urge you in the Lord Jesus to do this more and
more" (1 Thessalonians 4:1).

C. S. Lewis said it may be hard for an egg to turn into a bird, but it would be harder for it to learn to fly while remaining an egg. The finest athletes have rigid improvement routines, even during their off-season. And remember, the perfect Son of God "grew in wisdom and in stature, and in favor with God and man" (Luke 2:52).

In 2 Peter 1, the apostle calls us to increase, to "do this and more," and offers seven improvements to the faith you are perfecting in Christ:

- **Virtue.** Declare your faith by the way you work. In the church or in the world, be a walking and talking example of your beliefs.

- **Knowledge.** Move beyond a mere familiarity with God's Word. Mine truths from its books, chapters, verses, and lines until you discover gold.

- **Self-control.** Discipline the flesh. Think of the triggers that make you vulnerable to temptations and develop diversionary tactics.

- **Perseverance.** Consider every trial a place of learning and strengthening. Reflect on their underlying, positive purpose.

- **Godliness.** Aim to model Christ's life. Give a portion of your day to meditation, reading, or music that replaces dull duty with exuberant praise.

- **Kindness.** Strengthen your kingdom relationships through planned and specific, daily acts of mercy. Affirm at least one person each day.

- **Love.** Show unselfish, personal acceptance to someone of another culture or creed, and open an ongoing channel of communication to them.

When you have your eyes on a world harvest, you'll be diligent in readying yourself for the field. What's the next virtue you could add to your preparation for sharing the gospel?

God sees you as a compassionate servant who can see and hear and feel the needs of a lost world.

THINK ABOUT THIS

"While there remains one dark soul without the light of God, I'll fight—I'll fight to the very end!"
– William Booth

MY PRAYER

Lord, my priority is to be more like You. Show me what I can do to grow in Your grace, and help me to do it. Amen.

TRY IT

Name the point at which you are trying to grow, then ask someone to hold you accountable for it.

STORIES OF TRANSFORMATION

I Fell in Love in Kenya

Rebecca Denning | Volunteer, Kenya

The Call, *July/August/September 2017*

I fell in love in Kenya...with a dirty, hungry, home-less, 9-year-old boy. He was swinging on tree ropes near my home on the missionary compound at Tenwek Hospital. I could tell he was enjoying himself, smiling and pumping his legs hard as if it would swing him into a new life.

"Hey buddy, time to go home," I said. The pumping stopped, and he walked toward me, eyes on the ground. In broken English he said, "I have no parents." Another missionary walked by and I said, "Hey Jenny, this boy says he doesn't have parents." "Yeah, he told me the same thing earlier," she replied.

The neighbor's daughter, a Kenyan, was passing by so we asked her to translate. We discovered Emmanuel had been living on the streets and truly had no family. The three of us walked to a storage closet for orphans. We found a few outfits, a backpack, toiletries, and a teddy bear. For the next two days, Emmanuel slept at Jenny's house and even learned to ride a bicycle.

Emmanuel shared that he had been homeless for at least the last six months, but the gaps in his story suggested far longer. His mother had reportedly died of HIV when he was very young, and he didn't remember his father.

After two days of investigative work, no family could be found. It was now time to decide what to do with this precious little one. Peter, a dear Kenyan friend, helped us arrange for Emmanuel to be placed at nearby Mosop Children's Home, which doubles as a boarding school and has high standards for cleanliness, nutrition, academics, and medical care.

Peter and I loaded Emmanuel in the car, his new teddy bear peering out the side pocket of his backpack. Emmanuel was squirming and showing off his toothy smile, thrilled to be going to school.

As we pulled in the driveway, he practically jumped out of his seat in excitement, yelling, "Mosop-school! Mosop-school!" Children dressed in neat brown uniforms ran along the fence to greet us before teachers led us to a room where they gave Emmanuel an academic examination. It was determined he would be placed in Class 1 (the equivalent of first grade).

I hugged my little friend, told him I would see him tomorrow, and left him at that big school with people he had just met and a bunch of kids who I prayed would be nice to him. All night I thought about and prayed for that little guy.

I'd only known him for three days, but I felt like a part of me was missing. As I prayed, God brought three words to my mind: "God with us." Burdened with emotions, it took me a second to remember that Emmanuel means "God with us." Emmanuel has never been alone, forsaken, or homeless; and neither have I.

2

A CHOICE TO BE MADE

DAN SCHAFER

"No one can serve two masters."
— Matthew 6:24

I looked up and there he was. The suddenness of his appearance, and his proximity startled me. It wasn't my best judgment that put me into this situation, but now I had to make a choice. The stranger that was now right behind me was steering an 18-wheeler. We were both driving 70 mph in the fast lane on a slick, snow-covered freeway passing the rest of the traffic that was moving a more reasonable 55 mph – actually, the abruptness of his appearance indicated that he was driving much faster than 70 mph. I now had to make a choice; get out of the way or get run over. It was an easy decision. I changed lanes and let him pass.

Life is full of choices. And the most important one is who we will serve. Many protest, "I'm not serving anyone." But secular songwriter, Bob Dylan, got it right when he sang:

> But you're gonna have to serve somebody, yes indeed / You're gonna have to serve somebody / Well, it may be the devil, or it may be the Lord / But you're gonna have to serve somebody.
>
> — *http://bobdylan.com/songs/gotta-serve-somebody/*

"Do you not know that when you present yourselves to someone as slaves for obedience, you are slaves of the one whom you obey, either of sin resulting in death, or of obedience resulting in righteousness?" Romans 6:16

Jesus says we cannot serve two masters (Matthew 6:24). But we try. "How long will you hesitate between two opinions? If the Lord is God, follow Him; but if Baal, follow him." Elijah pleads (I Kings 18:21). Too many of us continue to want the pleasures of this world, even while we attempt to follow after Christ. But God tells us we must choose.

Why is this choice so important? Christian songwriter, Barry McGuire, once relayed an encounter with a detractor of his Christian faith. "You Christians, man, you've all been brainwashed." Barry agreed.

"…[But]…so have you…" Barry replied, "the only difference between all of us Christians and you is that we have all chosen who we want to wash our brains…mine were dirty, old sick brains anyways…they needed a scrub."

The world will offer us two altars at which to worship. We must choose only one of them. Only one of those choices offers us the cleansing we desperately need.

THINK ABOUT THIS

"'Cleanse your hands, you sinners; and purify
your hearts, you double-minded'
(James 4:8). It is the prayer of Christ for all that
are His, that they may be sanctified."
– Matthew Henry

MY PRAYER

Lord, purify my heart by faith and remove from me my double-mindedness. Amen.

TRY IT

List the three greatest challenges you face to serving the Lord, and then list the power that God provides to overcome each one.

STORIES OF TRANSFORMATION

The Two Altars

Nathan Metz | Missionary, Uganda

The Call, *July/August/September 2017*

"That one is for the men. This for the women. Those two smaller ones, the children."

Dusk was just minutes away, and we had a muddy van ride ahead. I saw the tarps, but I thought nothing of them. They appeared to be covering rocks—flat on the top with little jars and vessels tucked in around the base. As a new missionary, I knew very little about this place, just enough to feel fear. I trusted our pastors—a couple Kenyans and a few Ugandans—assuming they knew what they were doing since they were acting like guides.

They picked up the pace, so I followed suit. One turned to me as we scrambled back to our van, "Those altars, they are for sacrifice," one whispered from the corner of her mouth while glancing quickly over my shoulder back in the direction from which we had come.

Several years earlier, I stumbled across an altar of a very different kind. This altar has a story that began with a wedding. Floyd was a young man who waited nervously at the front of a small chapel in central Indiana. His fiancé,

Alberta, stepped happily down the aisle in a beautiful white gown.

Over 50 years later, a pew from that wedding chapel was strapped in the back of a red pickup while my father and I sketched out a plan to give the wood a second life. When finished, it looked like a kneeler...an altar. Its old pew shape still trimmed the sides and the top on the right and left.

It ended up at my house. I prayed there many times. There is no mistaking the vast difference between these two altars—one meant for evil, another meant for good. However, with all their differences, I find the similarities quite fascinating. Both altars are cared for as designated, sacred places. Both are intended to connect humanity with the supernatural. In both cases, humans approach the altar with sincerity, most always confident and expectant. I suspect Elijah saw this, too, on Mount Carmel as he faced the prophets of Baal. Two altars—vast in difference, striking in similarity.

In my ministry, I desire to see the lost come to the altar and seek the Lord in prayer. Yet, there is a great work that must occur before any man or woman comes to the altar of God. Before we kneel at a new altar, we must leave the one we've been using. A battle over the soul begins every time a person kneels at the altar of God before they've left their other altars. In the marshes of Uganda, in the twilight of that memorable day, I realized that my work in missions was somewhere between two altars—the death and the second life.

3

THE PLAN

STAN TOLER

"But one thing I do: Forgetting what is behind and
straining toward what is ahead, I press on toward
the goal to win the prize for which God has called
me heavenward in Christ Jesus."
– Philippians 3:13–14

What separates an also-ran from a winner? Or, a runner-up from a champion? Winners and champions link their plan to a purpose and plan to win. In the spiritual realm, God's plan for our victory was created before the beginning of time. "In him we were also chosen, having been predestined according to the plan of him who works out everything in conformity with the purpose of his will" (Ephesians 1:11).

Winners focus on a specific objective. No one plans for a second-place finish? It happens when a first-place plan isn't followed. R. A. Torrey said, "The reason why others succeed is because they have gained their victory on their knees long before the battle came." Winners in life and ministry have a specific objective in mind, based on an overall purpose. For believers, it is "the purpose of His will," becoming a disciple, being discipled, and discipling others. And every personal goal is focused on reaching that objective.

Winners conform to the purpose of the objective. Likewise, our life and ministry is focused on conformity with God's purpose. We are pliable to the working of God's will. We follow the blueprint of His Word and plan in keeping with the instruction of the Holy Spirit. Galatians 5:25, "Since we live by the Spirit, let us keep in step with the Spirit."

God sees you as a winner taking part in His winning plan. And winners claim victories of the objective in advance. The good news is that the One who works out everything has provided you with "everything [you] need for a godly life" (2 Peter 1:3). Forgiveness for sin, cleansing for sinfulness, and power for victory.

THINK ABOUT THIS

"We must be global Christians with a global vision
because our God is a global God."
– John Stott

MY PRAYER

Lord, I claim your purpose as my mandate and your
power as my motivation. Give me the vision, passion, and
energy to do your will. Amen.

TRY IT

Name the single most important thing God has for you
to do today, then do it.

STORIES OF TRANSFORMATION

Sacred Space in a School Infirmary
Christine Stanfield | Missionary, Uganda

The Call, *July/August/September 2017*

We use milestones collected in our hearts and minds to construct altars of remembrance. Sometimes we find ourselves building them in a most un-likely place.

One morning while working at Tenwek Hospital in Kenya, we were shocked to receive a phone call telling us our son, Chris, had a seizure in PE class at his boarding school. We quickly handed over duties, packed a bag, and started out on the long drive to be with Chris.

Upon arrival at the school infirmary, our hearts ached to see the many bumps and bruises and a cut from his fall against a wire fence and then down onto the ground. Chris was started on medication and needed to be monitored through the night. The nurse invited us to stay in the in-firmary with him. After a late supper, we settled in for the night.

I was startled awake as my spirit cried vehemently with-in me, "I am so disappointed in you, God! I trusted you to protect my son. I am very disappointed!" God joined my heart-space conversation. "I can handle your disappointment, but I have a question for you. Do you trust Me?"

"I do trust You, but I am disappointed."

"Do you trust Me?" I felt Him gently ask.

"I think I trust You. Why do You ask? You know the answer better than I."

"For what lies ahead for you and your family, for where I am leading you next, you must know if you trust Me. Do you trust Me?"

I invited God's Spirit to reveal what was in my heart. I saw incomplete trust. "Oh, God, I do trust You. Increase my faith to trust You more. Your Holy Spirit, always reminds me that I know I trust God. Whatever comes my way, I trust you, God."

Suddenly, within that room, my heart space became sacred ground and a holy quiet filled my being. Using every bump on my son's body as building stones, along with other mental stones from experiences past, I constructed an altar of remembrance in worship to God, whom I trust.

In the years since building that altar in the school infirmary, I have often gone to that sacred heart space to worship the God I trust. He was right. I needed to know that I know that I trust Him.

4

WAITING POWER

DAN SCHAFER

"Wait for the LORD; be strong and
take heart and wait for the LORD."
– Psalm 27:14

Mind boggling! Sitting in the sweltering heat of an Ugandan afternoon, I typed up and sent off an important email with several recipients. One of those recipients sat across the table from me, the others scattered around the world.

"Got it!" was the reply from my colleague seemingly before I lifted my finger from the sent button. How is it possible for that email to travel from my computer in the depths of Africa, across the continent, over the ocean to the heart of the US and then repeat the journey back, signaling its arrival into the inbox of my table companion in just a few seconds?

Not only is this possible, but it's occurrence is expected. If the email fails to make its appearance within those few acceptable seconds, our impatience grows. What's wrong?! We should have gotten that email 30 seconds ago.

Like our email, much of life is delivered at ultra-high speed. Many of us have grown accustomed to next day delivery from Amazon, instant downloadable movies, and an Uber "taxi" driver waiting just around the corner for our beckon call.

What a wonderful convenience these ultra-fast services and products bring to our lives. But writer Tim Elmore shares that there is an unexpected consequence of all this high-speed delivery. There is a significant danger that we will conclude that everything slow or that takes time is bad. Resulting in a practice of avoiding anything that takes time.

Why is this a danger to us? Simply put, we need the resistance that time consuming activities produce in our lives. Without it, we will not develop into the fully healthy persons God intends for us to be. It is these time-consuming activities that build character in our lives. For example, it is only as we practice waiting that we learn to be patient.

Perhaps you have seen the animated movie, *Wall-E*, where the humans no longer can walk because their muscles have all atrophied from their lack of use.

Waiting is important! Those that wait upon the Lord shall renew their strength. There is something about speeding through life that causes us to miss the power of God that is available to us. Elijah had to slow down from the events of Mount Carmel to hear the still small voice of God.

Such a voice can only be detected when we are standing still. Remember, God's voice wasn't detected in the wind that went rushing by. It's only when we learn to wait, that we can truly experience the strength of our God.

Again, I state that waiting is important. Waiting exercises the muscle of patience. Without the discipline of waiting, we will find ourselves woefully short on patience. Without patience — we will find ourselves short on love.

Love is patient (1 Corinthians 13:4). The mathematical law of equality informs us that we can flip this equation and restate it — patient [or patience] is love. The reality is that it requires a great deal of patience to live with and to love others. We must learn there are times when it is important to go slow because it builds the patience we need to love one another. And without that perseverance-developed patience we will not have what it takes to maintain the relationships with others that are needed to navigate life.

So, go ahead and enjoy the conveniences that bring speed to our lives, but don't write off everything that requires time and hard work, because those mental, spiritual, and/or emotional exercises are important to your mental, spiritual, and emotional health.

THINK ABOUT THIS

"Patience is bitter, but its fruit is sweet."

— Aristotle

MY PRAYER

Lord, teach me that some good things only come by waiting. Amen.

TRY IT

Try doing one thing today that someone might describe as the old fashion way and see what you might learn.

STORIES OF TRANSFORMATION

The Voices
Michael Johnson | Missionary,
Out of Nazareth (Pennsylvania)

The Call, *October/November/December 2016*

"You can see her in this room, Dr. Johnson." The caretaker of the women's shelter was glad that I had come to examine some of her residents. She politely escorted Felicia and me away from the crowded gathering into a small side room. "You will be able to hear them from here, but they won't be able to hear you talk with Felicia." All the residents were anxious to see the doctor; there just was not enough time to interview and examine them all that day.

This is a halfway house for women as they transition from jail or prison. Some are escaping violence in their homes or avoiding life on the streets, where they are forced to sell their bodies for food and shelter. This place is safe. Here, they can find the consistent comfort of blankets, caring providers, and, for today, a doctor visit.

Once we were alone, Felicia stood before me, her arms shaking like the limbs of a tree caught in a violent wind. She paced in place like a sprinter getting ready for a race. Then she opened up: "All I want is to stop the voices.

I have not had enough of my medicines since I was released from prison two weeks ago. They only gave me just enough medicine till I could see a doctor. I don't have insurance, and I don't know any doctor. I have been afraid of using all of my medicine because I did not want to run short. So, I only use it when I hear the voices. They are beginning to whisper now."

In order to keep the "voices" at bay, Felicia devised a plan to make her medications last a long time. She was desperate and knew a psychotic break would happen if she was not medicated soon. The scenarios for using prescription drugs are as varied and confusing as the stories of the almost two dozen women in the room we left behind.

I am no psychiatrist or psychologist, but I do know something about compliance when it comes to taking medicines. I never advise a diabetic to take medicine when nearing diabetic coma or a hypertensive patient to wait for onset of stroke to do likewise. I know that waiting to hear voices is not optimal therapy.

This type of care takes a team approach. I asked my wife, Kay, who is the clinic administrator, to pursue getting a release of medical records from Felicia's most recent emergency room visit. I reviewed the records and discussed the medication regimen with Dr. Pitts, our clinic director and clinical pharmacologist. Together, we consulted his wife, Pat, who is a practicing psychiatric nurse. She helped us formulate a plan that will readily renew the prescriptions.

I have studied and managed illnesses and diseases for a long time. However, providing healthcare for prostitutes and drug addicts is new. Then, of course, there are the people who have been recently released from incarceration and cannot afford their medications. Medications which, if they could afford them, would slow their organ failure, prevent infections, clear skin rashes, elevate their mood, and, of course, stop the voices.

My duties as a physician at Miriam Medical Clinics have brought me face to face with this reality. It's a rather complicated community, but as we gather around the common cause of health, I am reminded that God doesn't always call us to clean, safe ministries.

As I ponder which patient God will have me consult with next, I can rest in the assurance that He has a plan for each one. And I offer praise that for Felicia, the voices have been stopped. Maybe once they are gone completely, she will get the chance to hear His call.

5

PAIN AND THE CROSS

DAN SCHAFER

"Beloved, do not be surprised at the fiery
ordeal among you, which comes upon
you for your testing."
– 1 Peter 4:12 NASB

Run! But the command my brother issued to me was too late. I could not escape the danger that was just above my head.

When my mom and dad married, they moved from the big city to an isolated country home. My dad bought an old farm house that needed a lot of fixing up – for those that remember old sitcoms, think *Green Acres*. Among other challenges, it had no indoor plumbing, which, of course, meant we had an outhouse. This feature of our home wasn't brought into the modern era until I was about 7 or 8 years old.

And that was the location at which this scene played out on that day. I was somewhere around 5 years old at the time. My brother, 7 years my senior, had the facilities occupied. I was on the outside – let's just say – needing in. I was overcome with the feeling that I could not wait any longer, and so I began to use the door of the outhouse as a drum – pounding as hard as I could with both of my fists.

My pounding quickly produced a result, just not the one I expected. Unbeknownst to us all, bumblebees had taken up residence somewhere in or under the outhouse. They didn't appreciate their normally quiet residence being used as a percussion instrument, and they began expressing their displeasure by circling my head. I did what any self-respecting, 5-year old would do. I began swatting at them.

My brother emerged. Quickly assessed the situation and yelled his command. And we began running as though the starting bell at the Kentucky derby had just been sounded.

Being 7 years older than me, my brother outdistanced me quickly, leaving me and the bees to travel the 30 feet to the house together – just me and the bees. You guessed it, they were stinging me all the way. The bees presented me with upwards to 30 stings – one for each foot I ran. Eyes quickly swollen shut, moaning from the intense pain, and throwing up, I had forgotten all about my emergency need to enter the outhouse. I would recover, but I never forgot my lesson about what happens when you swat at bees.

Life is full of painful lessons, and we do our absolute best to avoid any situation that promises pain. But as the Proverb writer informs us, "Sometimes it takes a painful experience to make us change our ways" (Proverbs 20:30 GNT). The psalmist agrees, "Before I was afflicted I went astray, but now I keep Your word" (Psalm 119:67 NASB).

Romans 5:3 shows the character building qualities of pain. "And not only this, but we also exult in our tribulations, knowing that tribulation brings about perseverance; and perseverance, proven character; and proven character, hope." James also trumpeted the qualities of suffering, "Consider it all joy, my brethren, when you encounter various trials, knowing that the testing of your faith produces endurance" (James 1:2).

These verses and many others in the Bible clearly show us that pain and suffering can produce a positive result in our lives. The following story of transformation is painful. No one would have expected anything positive to have come from this situation, but God used it to open a missionary's eyes about the power of the cross.

THINK ABOUT THIS

"God whispers to us in our pleasures, speaks in
our conscience, and shouts in our pains."

– C.S. Lewis

MY PRAYER

Lord, don't let me resist the lessons You wish to teach
me through my pain and suffering. Amen.

TRY IT

Write down at least one lesson you have learned through
pain and/or suffering in your past.

Stories of Transformation

Do You See the Cross?
Shushan Richardson | Missionary, Creative Access

The Call, *July/August/September 2017*

In the days leading up to the trial that would eventually result in a not guilty verdict for the man who killed my youngest brother, I went on a private spiritual retreat. It was a time of prayer and seeking God.

In those days of quiet, I read the Bible and *Suffering and the Sovereignty of God* by John Piper. During those days, God brought me to the cross and helped me to see it. Before, I saw the cross as a picture of God's love, grace, and victory. My view was beautiful and joyful, but it was shallow. I realized that I had been missing the cost, cheapening the unimaginable suffering of Jesus. The cross is an amazingly powerful reminder that we are called to die, called to give up illusions that this world is fair and safe and just and easy.

It is a reminder that no matter the pain, difficulty, or cost, we are called to love and live and suffer as Christ did. I now see and feel the cross differently, overcome by the fullness of the vision. Worship for me has become all about the cross.

Like life, missions, is full of uncertainty. I had hoped to return to Ukraine, but the opportunity to serve with war-affected students drew me to the country of Georgia. There, I was presented with a new cross—the Georgian interpretation where the arms of the cross point downward. At first, I bristled at the strangeness and thought it was irreverent. But then I heard the beautiful story of a missionary to Georgia in the fourth century. She came to Georgia, sharing the gospel and living such a devout life that even the king took notice. She constructed a cross of grapevines, which she bound together with her hair. Eventually, she was able to lead the king to Jesus. Not only did he become a believer but also Georgia was a Christian country by the year 337. And the cross made of twisted grapevines remains a symbol of a life and a country dedicated to Christ.

When students from Iraq and Syria were unable to enter Georgia, the ministry was relocated to Lithuania. Here, too, the cross is a central theme. The Hill of Crosses in Lithuania is an awesome site. Hundreds of thousands of crosses have been placed on a small raised area outside of a city. The hill began as a memorial to soldiers lost in battle in the 1830s. It became a place of prayer for peace, and more crosses were erected. Under the Soviet Union, crosses and other Christian symbols were not permitted. Three times during the Soviet occupation, the crosses were destroyed. Yet under threat of punishment, Lithuanian people continued to sneak in in the dark of night to place crosses at this site, proclaiming their faith in God and praying for peace.

Recently, I was sitting with some students from Syria. We had the opportunity to speak with filmmakers who made a documentary about the Syrian refugee crisis. They asked the students how they are adjusting to Lithuania and what stereotypes they face as Muslims. One young man was quick to speak up. He said, "I will let my Muslim brothers answer, but first, I want to tell you that I am a Christian. Yes, Jesus is in Syria."

And Jesus is in Iraq, also, evidenced by the small wooden cross one of my Iraqi students wears proudly around his neck. Yes, life and missions are uncertain, but God is not. Wherever I go, God has already been there. I see the cross, and it asks if I am willing to do even more than love.

6

THE INTRUDER

DAN SCHAFER

"For as in Adam all die, so in Christ all
will be made alive."
— 1 Corinthians 15:22

Something had to be done! Two Sundays in a row, he had put fear into the hearts of those attending our rural church.

I was home alone on a weekday in the parsonage that sat across the parking lot from the church, and there he was. I found myself in a position where I knew I had to try to "take the intruder out." But I didn't have a weapon. I looked around and identified the only thing I thought might work, a few split logs from a stack of firewood.

He noticed me immediately as I stepped out the back-door. He didn't seem to be alarmed. I selected just the right size logs that I could chuck a good distance, and the battle was on. Man verses skunk.

It was a 30-minute epic battle. My initial wooden missiles fell short of the target, but got his attention. I reloaded my arms, and got closer. Finally, I made contact and stunned him.

I reloaded with larger logs and got closer still. Having made contact a few more times, I moved to even larger logs, at even closer range. Eventually, I was able to share with the people of the church that they no longer needed to worry about the skunk.

We all are locked in an epic battle with an intruder in our hearts - the nature of sin that was passed on to us from Adam (Romans 5:11-14). We are not equipped to fight this battle, let alone win it. Even the man or woman with the strongest commitment to self-control will, at best, only limit the devastating destruction of this inherited nature.

This intruder needs to be put to death to eliminate the threat. In Romans 6:6, Paul calls this intruder "our old self" revealing the truth that the intruder is us. The intruder is the worst version of our self, permanently corrupted by and enslaved to sin, with no way to escape.

But God can perform a miracle of new life in us that gives us the release from our old self that we need. "Knowing this, that our old self was crucified with Him, in order that our body of sin might be done away with, so that we would no longer be slaves to sin" (Romans 6:6).

We can only be freed from sin by the grace of God which is activated in our lives by accepting through faith (Romans 6:11) that our old self was crucified with Christ. When we do, the miracle of God's sanctifying power will do away with our body of sin, fill us with His Holy Spirit (Ezekiel 36:26,27, Acts 9:17), and we will be free to walk in the Spirit (Romans 8-4,11).

THINK ABOUT IT

"The message of God's desire to cleanse His people of the nature of sin is found from Genesis to Revelation."

– Louie Bustle

PRAYER

Lord, cleanse our hearts (Acts 15:9) of our old self, our inherited nature of sin, and help us to live the rest of our lives walking in Your Spirit. Amen.

TRY IT

Ask someone who has experienced this cleaning of the old nature about their experience with this grace of God.

STORIES OF TRANSFORMATION

Let Them Hear

Leatha Jenkins | Missionary, Papua New Guinea

The Call, *October/November/December 2015*

Would you expect somebody who has never been to school to speak multiple languages fluently? Not in our hometown in Ohio! Yet it is very common in the Highlands of Papua New Guinea. If you had grown up in the Highlands, the local dialect would be your first language, but you would also learn to recognize neighboring dialects and eventually Melanesian Pidgin, which is the trade language. The official language of PNG is English, but only the fortunate few who get higher schooling speak it fluently. Papua New Guinea is the most linguistically diverse country in the world. Papua New Guineans are very oral people!

Angal Enen, 'True Talk,' is the mother tongue of the Nembi and Wara Lai people, where the majority of our churches are located. One of our own missionaries, Ruth Tipton, researched and wrote the language script, then translated the New Testament into Angal Enen.

Recently, we were challenged to build on this translation. Why not record the translation? Good question, but we did not have a plan for that. Neither Butch nor I were

1) extremely technologically qualified, 2) we didn't have equipment, 3) there was no recording room, and 4) we do not speak Angal Enen. This request was going to take a leap of faith on our part, trusting that God would care for the details.

Guess what? The God who created languages is the God who inspired the Bible, and He broke down the logistical barriers one by one. We had a small hand-held recorder, readers from the village, a college student volunteer from America, a blanket-covered studio in the corner of an old medical building, and recent high school graduates to edit the recording on our computer.

Long story short: now we have a solar-powered audio unit that 'speaks' both the trade language and the local dialect. Many people who have not heard and understood the Word will now have that opportunity. However, even those who do read and speak multiple languages have a new advantage—hearing the Bible in their heart language. People like Silas, one of the young men on the editing team. Although Silas is fluent in English, he was impressed with how clearly he understood the Bible in his own language.

Thank you all for standing by us and helping provide the Word for the non-literate as well as the educated in their heart language. When God calls you to serve Him in a way that seems impossible, He is faithful to provide the resources you need.

7

BORN INTO WEALTH

STAN TOLER

"Whoever is generous to the poor lends to the LORD,
and he will repay him for his deed."
— Proverbs 19:17 ESV

According to *Forbes*, the eight wealthiest people in the world are, together, worth over four hundred billion dollars. That's more wealth than about half of the world combined.

Those who have struggled with meeting ends at month's end might fantasize about being born into one of those eight families. Or at least they wish they were distant cousins with standing invitations to their family gatherings.

Perhaps one or more of the eight wasn't born into wealth. Perhaps they climbed to the top of the financial hill through blood, sweat, and tears. Perhaps they were dot.com entrepreneurs whose companies made an initial public offering in the stock market and became overnight billionaires.

Two observations. One, you could have a billion dollars and still feel empty. Happiness isn't a bottom line in a portfolio. It was a wealthy man in the Bible named Nicodemus who approached Jesus and asked how to find what was missing in his life.

The second observation, when you give your heart to Christ, you are born-again into wealth. Wealth that all the accountants in the world couldn't tabulate. You are spiritually born into the kingdom of One who owns everything. The One who supplies your need from "the riches of his glory" (Philippians 4:19).

We need heaven's wealth more than earth's, but we can't even gain the world's wealth without heaven's assistance. "Remember the Lord your God, for it is he who gives you the ability to produce wealth." (Deuteronomy 8:18a)

The God of all wealth supplies the means for you to gain resources which can be used to meet the needs of that other half not represented in the eight wealthiest. And don't forget, the greatest poverty of the other half isn't just lack of money. They may have never heard about the riches of knowing Jesus as Savior.

God sees you as a manager of His resources to share the great riches of the kingdom to the world for which He gave His Only Son.

THINK ABOUT THIS

"We talk of the Second Coming;
half the world has never heard of the first."
– Oswald J. Smith

MY PRAYER

Lord, I treasure my salvation. I long to show my gratitude by spreading the wealth to others. Bring me opportunities to share your good news and make me attentive to them. Amen.

TRY IT

Share your testimony with at least one person today.

STORIES OF TRANSFORMATION

Building My Altar

Kelly Hallahan | Missionary, Uganda

The Call, *July/August/September 2017*

It's just two hours until my deadline. The girls are needy. The boys are playing video games. And this topic of building an altar in the midst of chaos is all too relevant. As a missionary, wife, and mom of four children, the demands on my time are many and urgent. I don't know what you face today, but I am sure the needs around you are urgent as well. We all need to build altars and meet with God; but, it isn't easy. I want to share three things I am learning about building an altar.

1. God knows my frame. He understands the demands on my time and how many times I have been up in the night with a needy baby. There are days when I don't have 20 minutes to sit by myself and "do my devotions." But on those days, He reminds me that just a glance from my eyes ravishes His heart (see Song of Songs 4:9). It's the attitude of my heart that matters. My desire to be alone with Him is a pleasing offering even when actually being alone with Him cannot happen. This is the altar of desire.

2. God accepts my living sacrifice (see Romans 12:1). As I cook, clean, and care for my family and neighbors, I can worship God. Everything that is done in love can be turned into worship. My motives are not always pure, and sometimes I serve with a spirit of resentment. When the cry of my heart is "for You…for You…for You…," this is the altar of diligence.

3. God delights in my neediness. I don't like asking for help. My American independence is a hindrance to my spiritual growth. He loves to meet my needs. And whenever I call out to Him in poverty of spirit or body, He comes (see Matthew 5:3); He fills me. This is the altar of dependence—it's one of His favorite places to meet me. My prayer today is that we will build an altar wherever we are in the world and meet with the living God. He created us to bear fruit for His kingdom, and, without Him, we can do nothing.

8

THE FEAR HANDICAP

DAN SCHAFER

"Perfect love drives out fear."
— 1 John 4:18

I will never visit Egypt!

It was much more than an irrational fear. The near deaths of three of my wife's uncles and their wives justified her feelings. They had spent 10 days or so in the Holy Land and planned a few more in Egypt. And that's where their trip went deadly wrong.

Sometime, after settling into the beds of their hotel, the streets flooded with violent protestors, and a battle erupted between the protesters and the security forces. The protesters set the hotel on fire, and hotel staff urgently woke them and led them to the rooftop. They fought their instincts, because it was clear it was more dangerous outside the hotel than inside this burning structure.

The battle continued. Without explanation, they were urgently instructed to head back down. At times, crawling under the smoke, they made their way into a walled courtyard outside the hotel.

Safety seemed far from them in both time and distance. Then, without warning a UN tank broke through the wall to provide a rescue. Every family member was whisked out of harms' way.

But an indelible impression had been made, and my wife made two promises: 1) She would never go to Egypt. 2) The first thing she would do in a hotel was to locate the emergency exit. In the intervening 30 years since this incident, she had faithfully kept both promises.

Until last year.

A new ministry initiative to the Greater Middle East resulted in an invitation to Egypt for us both. Disappointed, knowing she would never go, I relayed the invitation.

Shockingly, she gave no immediate response. Instead, a prayer meeting ensued. Over the next two days God spoke, and we booked our tickets to Egypt.

On Easter Sunday, eight days before our flight, two churches were bombed in Egypt, killing dozens. Her feelings of incredible fear returned.

Our Egyptian friend, who was accompanying us on this trip, called my wife. "I can't promise you that you will be safe, but I promise I will die first." Another prayer meeting ensued. The result was the same. We were going to Egypt.

We arrived at our hotel in Cairo. We climbed into bed and I turned out the lights. Then it struck me.

"Did you check for the emergency exit?" "No," she answered. I inquired further, "Do you want me to check?" "That's not necessary," she responded, and she drifted off to sleep.

Thirty years of a fear-driven habit disappeared in a moment of God's peace.

The next day, I relayed the story to our friend. That night, he requested she share her account with the Christian leaders we were planning to meet. It created an amazing bond with them.

Two days later, we met with the leader of these leaders. They asked for her to repeat her story for their superior. She could hardly tell the story because they excitedly interrupted her to help her tell it.

The fear that had been nearly a life-long handicap, had become an advantage for ministry.

THINK ABOUT IT

"We have nothing to fear but fear itself."
– Winston Churchill

PRAYER

Lord, use what Satan has intended to use to paralyze me to bring about good for others. Amen.

TRY IT

List 3 fears or concerns you have and then list how God could use them for good.

STORIES OF TRANSFORMATION

Rekindled Vision

Jon and Lindsay Birkey | Missionaries,
American Indian Field (Arizona)

The Call, *December 2017*

We were at our wits' end. Raising financial support is HARD! We were moving at a snail's pace. Despite our efforts, we did not make much headway. We were starting to feel down.

And, as we all know, this is when Satan likes to creep in; and he did. He attacked us hard. We began looking at the progress we had made since we left the field previous. We had only raised about 57 percent of our monthly support, and the devil used this number to make us feel more discouraged.

After all the traveling, speaking, and time invested, we had little to show for it. Or so we thought. As the doubt began to creep in, we thought: can we really do this? Maybe this just isn't for us.

So, we revisited our callings and how God was preparing us—even at early ages—for our roles at Southwest Indian Ministries Center in Arizona. What God had done and what God was doing were now our focus, not doubt or lack of funding.

God began revealing to us steps we could take and people we could go to for help in the process. We felt a weight lifted off our shoulders. We knew things were in God's hands, not our own; and we knew that He provides in His timing, not ours. In the week following this shift in thinking, God helped us raise almost $400 in new monthly support! We may never fully know or see firsthand how God worked in the unproductive months, or what He did in the hearts of those we have met since.

Maybe someone we spoke to had surrendered their life to the Lord, or dedicated their life to missions. Maybe seeds were planted for the kingdom that we will not fully comprehend until we all get to heaven. But two things remain certain— God's Word never returns void, and we don't believe His callings on our lives return void either.

We sorted through camp pictures for a VBS project at Jon's home church. They were raising money to donate to our ministry. We decided to show them a picture of a camper each day for every $25 dollars they raised. Lindsay's task was to find pictures that show what our camps and campers are like.

As she looked through the hundreds of photos on Facebook, God pulled at her heartstrings. "I CANNOT leave these children!" Lindsay thought. "Everyone in their lives has left them. Their mothers or fathers might be gone. Other family members and friends might be gone.

We HAVE TO continue sharing Jesus with these kids! We
HAVE to go back!"

And so, it is with this rekindled vision of what God
has done and what He's continuing to do that we move
forward—in His strength, on His time.

9

CONFUSED WITH THE DRUNKARD

DAN SCHAFER

*"Since we are living by the Spirit, let us follow the
Spirit's leading in every part of our lives."*
– Galatians 5:25

They're drunk!

The derogatory remarks were directed at my friend and me. I was unbearably cold, and rain soaked, but I resolutely stood there in the dark holding up my friend firmly by his belt just a few inches off the ground. We had just come down out of the Sierra Nevada mountains viewing the majestic redwood trees in the most amazing snow that gently glided down, decorating each branch, turning these already regal trees into a magical scene.

Longing to stay and extend this moment, we recognized that darkness was falling, and we needed to get down off the mountain. We began our journey down.

As we arrived on the edge of a small village, we crossed the line where the snow turned to rain. We pulled into a small shopping center to remove the snow chains on our tires that the officials had required us to use to go up the mountain.

The chain came off easily from the first tire, but the chain on the second one unhooked on only one side and fell behind the tire in this half-released position. It was now out of our reach in its new location. It could only be assessed by laying on the ground so that we could reach behind the tire. Normally, this would not be a problem, but due to the rain, there was at least an inch of standing water in front of that tire.

I had a plan. I grabbed my friend by his belt and lowered him face down and held him just a couple inches off the ground while he attempted to reach behind the tire to unhook the chain. A shop owner was watching this unfold from one of the shop windows of this center. He didn't recognize that we were having trouble with a tire chain, he only saw this very unusual scene of two men standing in the rain with one of them dangling above the ground by his belt. His conclusion – they must be drunk.

At that moment, the shop owner's wife pulled up in her car to pick him up. She got out of the car and started to approach our location. He concluded that his wife was unknowingly approaching a situation that would put her in danger. Opening the door to his shop, he released his guard dog. The dog quickly ran to our location to protect its master's wife. Suddenly my friend was eyeball-to-eyeball with this growling dog.

Moments later the owner appeared at the dog's side, and we successfully convinced him we were sober and just trying to unhook the tire chain. He directed his wife to pull her car around and shine its lights on our location, so we could finish our task and be on our way.

This wasn't the first time that God's servants were accused of being drunk. On the day of Pentecost, Peter and the other disciples were filled with the Holy Spirit and mistakenly perceived to be drunk on wine. In Acts 2:15-17 Peter declares, "For these men are not drunk, as you suppose, for it is only the third hour of the day; but this is what was spoken of through the prophet Joel: 'And it shall be in the last days,' God says, 'That I will pour forth of MY Spirit on all mankind; And your sons and your daughters shall prophesy, And your young men shall see visions, And your old men shall dream dreams.'"

May we all be so filled with the Holy Spirit that we will see the visions of God and dream His dreams. May our dreams be so great that others will think them so fanciful that they will confuse our words with the babblings of a drunken man or woman.

THINK ABOUT THIS

"Pay attention to your dreams for they
are letters from God."
— Jewish Proverb

MY PRAYER

Lord, fill me full of your Spirit and fill me with your
visions and your dreams. Amen.

TRY IT

Write down a dream that God has given you through
His Spirit.

Stories of Transformation

Burning Bush Moment

Viktor Rózsa | Missionary, Hungary

The Call, *July/August/September 2017*

What was your burning bush moment?

In Exodus 3:1-12, Moses met God in a mysterious way on Mount Horeb. The experience of the burning bush changed his life forever. The call on Moses' life required him to wrestle with God's mission. As he spent those years in the wilderness and learned about God, he was challenged to take his relationship with the God of his forefathers to the next level. Moses had to sacrifice his comfortable life of being a shepherd, for 40 years in the wilderness, surrendering his life to a higher call so that God's mission could be fulfilled to His chosen people.

I clearly remember the burning bush moment of my life. Though it was not as mysterious as Moses' experience, it changed my life forever. While I was attending military high school, I gave my life to Christ through the ministry of missionaries in Hungary. At that time, I was set on a course of life that guaranteed a job, financial security, and a prestigious career in the Hungarian Air Force and ultimately in NATO. I was fine with being a Christian in the

Hungarian Air Force. Little did I know when I gave my life to Christ that there would be a deeper call one day.

My burning bush experience came between my junior and senior years of high school when I lived in Great Britain during the summer to improve my English language abilities. While I was there, God asked me to enter full-time ministry. I struggled with sacrificing a future that I thought was the greatest thing on the face of the earth. I had to surrender to God's leading so that His call upon my life could be fulfilled for His purpose in His mission. At the time, surrendering my future career to God was hard. However, as I have followed Him in this deeper call for His mission, God has shown His faithfulness time after time.

It was hard for Moses to process his call into God's mission. Like him, I had to face a very serious process of sacrifice and surrender to His call to serve Him in His mission in Hungary. However, when God calls someone, He makes a way. He is alongside that person the entire journey.

10

THE CONFRONTATION

DAN SCHAFER

"Every good thing given and every perfect
gift is from above, coming down
from the Father of lights."
– James 1:17 NASB

The scene was set for a confrontation, but I was caught off guard when it occurred. The object at the center of the conflict seemed innocent enough. The individuals involved were typically and often engaged in joyful, pleasant interactions.

Then the offending moment occurred. I reached across the table and attempted to lift a French fry from my grandson's McDonald's Happy Meal. I was greeted with a very unhappy declaration: "That's mine!"

I suggested that it was okay for him to share with me. My logic was countered with greater insistence as to who was the owner of the fry in question.

It was time for a lesson from Grandpa.

I backed away from the fries momentarily and asked my grandson a question: "Who bought your Happy Meal today?" He looked at me with that look that indicated he knew something was coming that he might not like. "You did, Grandpa."

"So, then that makes me the owner of all the French fries, doesn't it?" There was no response. I continued. "And as the owner of those fries, I gave them to you. Now don't you think you should allow Grandpa to have some back?"

A smile came across his face, and he spun the bag of fries around toward me. I completed the motion that had earlier been so abruptly ended, lifting out three fries. "That's all I need. Thank you," I said. My grandson returned to his normal happy self, and I was pleased that this afternoon in McDonald's, my grandson had learned an important lesson in life.

But as I look back on that interaction, I have a nagging question. Have we all learned this same lesson in our Christian walk? I wonder how often God reaches toward us to take something we possess to use for His purposes and we abruptly cry out, "No, that's mine," forgetting that "the earth is the Lord's, and everything in it" (Psalm 24:1).

All too often, our actions seem to indicate we have forgotten that everything we have really belongs to the Lord, and He has simply given it to us to manage for Him. We forget that He is the true owner. And we resist His attempts to take something in our possession to use for His kingdom purposes.

It is time for us to spin around the bag of our possessions and face it toward God, allowing Him to lift out whatever He wants. And when we will do this, we will experience the incredible joy that comes from being a good steward. That joy will flood our lives.

THINK ABOUT THIS

"We all are born with a bent toward selfishness, the very essence of the nature of sin that is passed down to us from Adam. It causes us to lose sight of where our possessions originate and who is their true owner."

- Dan Schafer

MY PRAYER

Help me to remember that all I possess is really Yours. Let me be faithful with what You have given me to use for Your kingdom and to benefit others. Amen.

TRY IT

Share your testimony with at least one person today.

STORIES OF TRANSFORMATION

Cynthia's War Room
Carolyn Wade | Missionary, Kenya

The Call, *July/August/September 2017*

The movie *War Room* is about a woman who prays faithfully from her closet? My Kenyan friend Cynthia (name changed) was so inspired by that movie that she created a similar space in her own home.

I first met Cynthia in 2011, when we met with several girls who wanted to leave the sex industry. She has continued ministering to them since that time. Cynthia has a missionary heart, encouraging and supporting widows and other needy people in her community.

I knew the Holy Spirit was guiding me to mentor Cynthia. She was in crisis at the time. She and her children had been victims of physical and emotional abuse by the children's father. The chief had given a letter of warning to the father, and Cynthia left the home with the four boys. She had been praying for a resolution in the family.

Cynthia related how the movie *War Room* had impacted her prayer life. She learned that there is power in secret prayer. She had constructed a wardrobe in which to hang her clothes, and this wardrobe became her prayer closet. Each time she wanted to pray, she removed the clothes from the wardrobe and went inside to pray. She poured out her heart to the Lord about all that concerned her and her children during those precious moments of prayer.

The family has since moved to a larger home, and Cynthia created a new space for prayer. This "closet" is a curtained-off area of her bedroom. Now, all four of her boys join her in bringing requests before the Lord and posting them on the "War Room" wall. When the Lord gives an answer, they mark the response. The answers to prayer are flowing!

One day, her son Joshua went into the closet to thank the Lord for the cup of plain tea they were drinking. He told the Lord that he wanted to be grateful for it, because surely the Lord had chosen to give their sugar to someone who needed it more. He was trusting the Lord to supply for their needs. Soon after, there was a knock at the door. A woman handed Cynthia two kilos (about four and a half pounds) of sugar and a large bag of tea leaves. Later that day, three packets of milk were brought to the house. The answered prayer came about in the supply of all the ingredients needed for a proper cup of tea!

Cynthia has started a small shop selling produce, French fries, soap, and matches. Her boys are in school with fees paid by Cynthia. Joshua was chosen the leader for the Christian Union at his high school, leading devotions each Friday.

Helping former sex workers earn clean money and discipling them are two of Cynthia's goals. Recently, on her birthday, nine girls accepted Christ as their Savior and left the sex industry. Four of them are now washing clothes for other women, and Cynthia is working to encourage them all in their new lives.

11

DON'T SETTLE

DAN SCHAFER

"If God is for us, who can be against us?"
– Romans 8:31

We find ourselves in the midst of a grand scheme – an elaborate web of lies that leave us struggling to know the truth. The originator of the deception, the Father of Lies, has one purpose – to devour us as a roaring lion would his prey. Satan would have us believe we are a defeated church; void of power; no longer able to transform our world.

In blitzkrieg style, his deception, the alternate reality he is creating is delivered via a steady barrage of cultural "truths" that are defacing our long-held values and eroding the very bedrock on which we have stood as a nation for over two centuries.

But none of what Satan proclaims as reality is true!

The real truth is found in Matthew 16:18, ESV, "…I will build my church, and the gates of hell shall not prevail against it." That is not the depiction of a defeated church, it's the revelation of a triumphant church; a church experiencing victory over Satan and his kingdom of darkness. It is a church bringing restoration and wholeness to lives of individuals that had been imprisoned behind the gates of hell.

Don't misunderstand who is on the defensive. Think about it, "gates" are not an offensive weapon. This scripture reveals that Satan, in a last-ditch effort, has erected gates around those he has imprisoned in darkness to keep them from being exposed to the good news of Jesus Christ. But the ineffectiveness of those gates is here declared: "they shall not prevail," they cannot withstand the advance of the Church.

When the church marches on the gates of hell, it will overpower them, setting free those whom Satan has enslaved.

So why does it seem to some that the church is in retreat? It is simple. The church – the people of God – have stopped being the church. They have stopped advancing on hell because Satan's menacing roar has convinced them they are on the losing side.

This is Satan's only possible winning strategy. Defeated by the Cross, he can only win if the church doesn't engage him in battle.

Too many Christians have believed his lies and are sitting on their hands. They see the gates of hell from where they sit – watching prisoners being dragged into a hellish prison – they do nothing. Not because they don't care, but they are convinced there's nothing they can do.

But Matthew 16:18 is a call to action – to ignore the lies.

If you don't want to settle for the lies of Satan; if you don't want to settle for a life that is less than God's best for you, then rise and join us at WGM and become a Gate-Crasher. Rise up and join us to declare God's truth – "the gates of hell shall not prevail against us."

THINK ABOUT THIS
"Give me the love that leads the way."
– Paul Rees

MY PRAYER
Lord, don't let me settle for anything less than God's best for my life. Amen.

TRY IT
Name 3 things that Satan has tempted you to settle for instead of God's best.

STORIES OF TRANSFORMATION

My Log Cabin Calling

Bonnie Gouge | Regional Director,
South America and Iberia

The Call, *December 2017*

W hy do you do what you do? I do what I do because God made it very clear to me that He was
calling me to serve Him. In the spring of 1980, we loaded
up our worldly goods and our two babies and moved to a
16 x 30-foot log cabin in Casey County, Kentucky.

Electricity stopped at the neighbor's house two miles
away, and our "running water" sloshed out of the buckets
as we ran from the pump to the cabin. Rain pouring off the
roof became our shower. But we loved our homestead and
embraced life in rural Kentucky.

Looking for a church home, we settled in the small
congregation of Atwood Chapel United Methodist. At the
end of a revival service message, our young pastor, Dave,
stood up. "God is speaking to someone about their gifts or
a calling. Please come and pray." We headed to the altar.

Later, the pastor joined us at the cabin, as we continued to pray. With the oil lamps burning, we sensed the
presence of Almighty God as we poured out our hearts in
prayer and earnestly sought Him. Afterward, Pastor Dave

said, "Do you remember the first time I visited you at this cabin? I went home and told my wife, 'I don't know who those people are or what they are doing here, but God has a call on their lives for missions.'" Ron quickly assured him that he was not missionary material. Yet, we were certain that God had met with us and that He had set us apart for His service.

Seeking confirmation, and it seemed that every time I opened the Bible, I found verses like Luke 10:2, "The harvest truly is great, but the laborers are few."

That winter, the pastor announced the district was sponsoring a work team to Haiti. Ron was drawn to this opportunity. As he built a school in the mountains of Haiti, he experienced what it could be like to serve God in missions.

He came back from Haiti saying YES to God. We spent a year seeking the Lord and researching missions organizations and were discouraged that we did not meet any of the requirements. In desperation, Ron cried out to God, "Please reveal Yourself to me. Send someone with a word from You so that I know that You are leading."

The next night at the hospital where Ron worked as a lab tech, a local pastor, whom Ron had met at the hospital, stopped by to chat. Ron shared his desperation to hear from God. The pastor pointed his finger at Ron, saying, "God is definitely working in your life, and you had better get yourself to college and prepare for whatever He has for you."

I wasn't so sure. I was a country girl at heart, and I didn't want to say goodbye to our cows, rabbits and chickens and move to Asbury University to study.

But one night, I climbed the wooden ladder to our loft bedroom, blew out the last oil lamp, and snuggled in to read the Bible with a flashlight. Turning to Habakkuk 3, I read, "Though the yield of the olive should fail and the fields produce no food, Though the flock be cut off from the fold and there be no cattle in the stalls, Yet I will exult in the LORD, I will rejoice in the God of my salvation. The LORD God is my strength."

God assured me that He was my God and my strength and that my joy did not depend on anything but Him.

12

BE THERE

STAN TOLER

"You will be my witnesses in Jerusalem,
and in all Judea and Samaria, and
to the ends of the earth."
— Acts 1:8

If you had a world globe as a child, you probably remember spinning and then stopping it by putting your finger on a country or region. John Stott wrote "We must be global Christians with a global vision, because our God is a global God."

As Christ-followers, His mission is our mission, and His heart is our heart. Our compassion must include our community, but its reach is even farther. Like Wesley, the world is our parish.

Spiritually, it's possible to be in two places at once. You can be *here* in person and *there* in spirit. Spin the globe—and then associate a certain country or region with a known missions organization, field, and staff. And be there.

Be there with the staff. Pray for God's supply in the details of their ministry. Contact them and encourage them. Join their support team. Remember them on holidays and special days.

Be there with the work. Learn about the specific ministries of organizations and staff. Pray for God's wisdom and supply in their operation. Donate time onsite if possible. Inquire about specific needs and give toward them.

Be there with the security. Learn about regional security challenges. Pray daily for field and staff onsite protection. Be a prayer warrior against the devil's evil intent. Claim God's promises over the work.

Be there with the provision. Learn about specific needs. Join the supply line. Raise and give funds to support programs and personnel. Form prayer teams and pray for God's provision. Sponsor an international or national worker.

God sees you in a place where you are needed. And He sees as you, in your heart, travel throughout the world in prayer.

THINK ABOUT THIS

"There is not a square inch in the whole domain
of our human existence over which Christ, who is
Sovereign over all, does not cry, Mine!"
– Abraham Kuyper

MY PRAYER

Lord, wherever the name of Jesus is being preached,
count on me to be there. Start a fire in my heart for the
places where you need me the most, and I will pray, give,
or go. Amen.

TRY IT

Locate a missions directory and pray for at least three
missionary families by name today.

STORIES OF TRANSFORMATION

Anchoring at an Altar

Jessica Hogan | Volunteer, Honduras

The Call, *July/August/September 2017*

The alarm sounds early, waking Ivan from his slumber. He slips out of bed, rubs his eyes, and makes his way to the chapel in the early morning darkness. A rooster crows to announce the new day, and the crickets continue their steady chirping cadence.

He opens the chapel doors and turns on the lights, already joined by a few others who chose to give up some sleep. This small group calls themselves the Remnant of Intercession.

Ivan walks to the front and faces the altar. The students at Escuela El Sembrador (School of the Sower) in Honduras will be waking up in an hour, and the chaos of the day will begin. But for now, he embraces the stillness. For now, it is only God and him, sharing a quiet moment.

On his knees, he bows his face to the floor.

He breathes.

He begins to pray.

Ivan is the residential life counselor with a missionary's heart at El Sembrador. Caring for over 80 residential boys is a daunting task, which is why Ivan decided last year to dedicate the first hour of the day to prayer.

"I wanted to give God the first moments of the day," he said. "In that time, I could give all my burdens to God, and it helped me begin my work with new strength." Over time a small group of students joined him, and together they prayed for their classmates, for El Sembrador employees, and for the leadership of the school.

The boys have a routine of school in the morning, work in the afternoon, and studying and playing in the evening. From the time the bell in the dining hall is first rung in the morning, Ivan's work is nonstop until the boys share a devotional and then go to bed at night. It is very important for Ivan to set aside some time every day to enjoy the calm that comes with resting in God's presence. These moments are an anchor for Ivan so that he is ready to face whatever life brings him.

13

YOUR STORY

STAN TOLER

"One thing I do know. I was blind but now I see!"
– John 9:25

The nameless young man in the New Testament told a powerful story of Christ's healing. Like him, you have a story. Your experience is the raw materials of that story. It can powerfully encourage and guide your family or social network.

Trapped in a discussion between religious zealots who tried to discredit Jesus, and incredulous community and family members, the young man, who had been born blind, told his story in seven words: "I was blind but now

I see!" He spoke from his heart, spontaneously. He didn't need a script to impact his world and worlds to come. And neither do you.

Your story is the *life-changing thing* Jesus did for you? You might say, "He *saved* me." You were lost, and He found you. You were captive, and He set you free.

Or, your story might be one of *healing*. You were sick, and He provided the remedy. You were broken in spirit and He put you back together.

Your story may be one of *spiritual victory*. You were bound by sinfulness, and He cleansed you. You were helpless in your spiritual walk, and He filled you with the power of his Holy Spirit.

Your story may be *financial.* You were captive to debt, and He showed you the way out. You were down to your last penny, and He miraculously supplied what you needed.

"That's my story, and I'm sticking with it!" is an expression that could go either way. But when you say it based on what Jesus did for you, it's a story that is as credible as Christ, and as powerful as His grace.

God sees you as a storyteller of grace to the world.

THINK ABOUT THIS

"I have but one candle of life to burn, and
I would rather burn it out in a land filled with
darkness than in a land flooded with light."
– John Keith Falconer

MY PRAYER

Jesus, help me put into words the things you have done silently in my heart. May I use opportunity to give You glory. Amen.

TRY IT

Write down your "elevator pitch" for the gospel: your own testimony in three sentences or less.

STORIES OF TRANSFORMATION

A Case for Immigrants

Michael Guilliams | Missionary, North America

The Call, *July/August/September 2016*

The Arabic lady was sitting alone on a bench while I was at the park with our boys. As a man, it would normally be improper for me to speak to a Muslim woman; however, God prompted me to speak to her. What came next was a surprise. As she talked in broken English, I began to see a picture of a heart that was lonely from years of a hard life and that was weighed down with many burdens.

She began talking about her family, friends, and a desire to find a job and to learn English. We talked for over an hour, and a door opened for me to become part of her life. My wife started to meet with her to help her learn English, and a friendship has developed as we have simply shared life with her.

From driving her to job interviews to helping her family move, it has been an education to see what difficulties people face when coming to another country. In the media, there has been a lot of talk about immigrants: what should be done and what shouldn't be done with people coming from the Middle East and surrounding countries. I would like to make a case for immigrants, that they be seen as souls to be won for Christ.

For many years I have heard people say, "I could never go to another country to share Christ with others." In God's wisdom, He has now made the people from other countries our new neighbors.

As I have traveled the country, it has become clear that the United States is changing at a rapid pace. For many, the possibility of people coming from other countries to settle within their own neighborhoods is a reality. The question is, how do we respond to these ever-increasing numbers of people?

The answer is to not look at them as a burden, but to view them as people who need to hear about the love of Christ. Just as we have shown love and compassion to our Lebanese friend, it is important for us, as believers, to love and care for those who need our help.

The path to making a difference starts with meeting needs: teaching English, providing food, being a friend, or even providing mechanical assistance. In simple ways, you can make a difference in the life of an immigrant. As we sort out the differences in culture, class, and expectations placed upon us by our experiences, it is important to remember that we all have the same basic needs: to be fed, to have purpose, and to be loved. And everyone needs to know that there is forgiveness and healing in the name of Jesus.

14

LIVING PROOF

STAN TOLER

*"I thank my God through Jesus Christ for all of
you, because your faith is being reported
all over the world."*
— Romans 1:8

What in the world are people saying about you?
They are *saying* what they are *seeing*. You are
living out your life story. Every day, everywhere you go, the
pages of your story are being "read" by those around you.
The apostle Paul commended Christ followers in the pagan
culture of Rome for living a holy lifestyle. But he wasn't the
only one to notice; their story was being communicated

outside their community, across their nation, and around the world.

They were modeling their beliefs. They preached the gospel message in their words and actions. People knew what they stood for by noticing for what they were taking a stand. Salvation and sanctification through Christ aren't just historical beliefs, they are practical applications. Street-level beliefs.

Those Christ-followers were translating His words in familiar settings. People understood what Christ said, and what He could do, by what He was doing in their lives.

They were sowing His truth in ready soil. They were living answers to people who only had questions about the activities of their culture. Day by day, action by action, they were telling the spiritually hungry where to find spiritual food. Their prayers were a pleasant aroma. Their deeds formed spiritual paths. "So God can point to us in all future ages as examples of the incredible wealth of his grace and kindness toward us, as shown in all he has done for us who are united with Christ Jesus" (Ephesians 2:7 NLT).

God sees you as a model of His mercy and grace.

THINK ABOUT THIS

"When a new Christian stands up and tells how God has revolutionized his or her life, no one dozes off."

– Jim Cymbala

MY PRAYER

Lord, thank you for using my life as a witness of your saving grace. Let my light shine brightly today, so that others may know of your glory. Amen.

TRY IT

Review the last twenty-four hours and ask, "Did others see Christ in me?"

STORIES OF TRANSFORMATION

Is It Worth Sowing Seeds among Troubled Kids?

Tracy Dubois | Copyeditor
with Terry and Colleen Hawk | Regional Directors,
Caribbean, Central and North America, and Mexico
The Call, *January/February/March 2017*

When you plant pumpkin seeds in your garden, you expect to harvest pumpkins. If you plant sweet corn seeds, you expect to eat sweet corn soon. However, when it comes to sowing the seeds of God's love in the hearts of children, the harvest is not always immediate or what you expect.

- Train up a child in the way he should go, and when he is old he will not depart from it. (Proverbs 22:6 RSV)

- According to www.churchleadership.org, the average age when people become Christians has steadily dropped over the years. Roughly 80 to 85 percent of people who become Christians do so by:
  - the age of 18 (1978)
  - the age of 16 (1988)
  - the age of 15 (1998)
  - the age of 14 (2008)

Didier is living proof of this promise and these statistics. He was born in Honduras and lived with his grandparents. The family was very poor, forcing Didier to dig through garbage to find food. His grandma died when he was 8, and Didier started getting into trouble. Three years later, Didier was sent to Escuela El Sembrador by his grandpa, who was unable to care for him. Didier studied at El Sembrador from 1993 to 1997, when he completed sixth grade.

Didier accepted Christ during a church service at El Sembrador when he was 13. Jorge Pacheco, a former El Sembrador student who was serving as a counselor at the school, helped lead Didier to the Lord. Terry and Colleen Hawk directed the school at the time.

Didier walked away from his faith and moved to the U.S. But, by God's grand design, Didier returned to the truths he learned at El Sembrador. He and his wife, Lourdes, began attending church and decided to renew their commitments to God and raise their two young sons in His light.

In May 2016, at the age of 35, Didier was baptized by Jorge—the same man who helped lead him to the Lord in 1997— in a Hispanic church in New Orleans. The Hawks were present for this grand celebration.

"It was a special God moment when Jorge baptized Didier," Terry and Colleen recalled. "May this be a call for people to invest in the lives of young children, because you never know what the seed you plant will bring to harvest. It is truly worth it!"

Jorge added, "Always give yourselves fully to the work of the Lord, because you know that your labor in the Lord is not in vain (1 Corinthians 15:58b)."

"I feel very blessed walking with the Lord," shared Didier. "I have established a Christian home and have my own construction company. Lourdes teaches a Sunday School class, and I am waiting for the Lord to show me what He wants me to do in the church."

15

IN DEFENSE OF THE FAITH

STAN TOLER

"Always be prepared to give an answer to everyone
who asks you to give the reason for the hope that
you have. But do this with gentleness and respect."
— 1 Peter 3:15

Apologetics doesn't mean specializing in apologies. Its origin is the Greek word meaning "verbal speech in defense." Well-known Christian apologists who have defended the faith include such scholars as Paul the apostle, Augustine, Justin Martyr, Thomas Aquinas, and John Wesley. Modern defenders of the faith include such authors as Lee Strobel and Josh McDowell.

Have you considered that as a follower of Christ, your name is on the list? That's what the apostle Peter suggests, "Give an answer to everyone who asks." As a Christian, your story begins with your belief that Jesus Christ is who He said He is: the virgin born Son of God, the Savior, the way to God, the truth of His Word, and the only source of eternal life. You not only accepted that truth, you promised to live by it—and defend it.

In a world where followers of over four-thousand religions boast of a way to God, Christianity stands alone. And it stands alongside a Savior with an empty grave behind Him, and a promised, final victory over sin and the devil before Him. Be ready to defend the faith. How?

First, prepare. "Put on the full armor of God, so that when the day of evil comes, you may be able to stand your ground" (Ephesians 6:13). Know what you believe about—

- Sinning against God,

- Salvation through faith in Christ,

- The source of holy living in the power of the Holy Spirit, and

- The authority and relevance of Scripture.

Then, as Peter said, be ready to defend it "with gentleness and respect." Quiet persuasion is a far more effective defense than loud demonstration. We are known not only by our belief, but by our love. God sees you as a scholar who is continually researching the truth of His Word.

THINK ABOUT THIS

"We are debtors to every man to give others the gospel in the same measure in which we have received it."
– Phineas F. Bresee

MY PRAYER

Lord, you are my source of wisdom and strength. I want to speak a good word in your name, but I need your guidance to do so. Give me conviction, courage, and opportunity. Amen.

TRY IT

From the bulleted list above, choose one topic and write your "defense" of the gospel.

STORIES OF TRANSFORMATION

God's Influence Showcased

Erin Curtis | Writing Intern with Bob Margaron |
Missionary, The Center (California)

The Call, *October/November/December 2016*

The Center, a community outreach, in Stockton, California, is catalyzing powerful shifts in the lives of people. Evidence of God's transforming power is touching many individuals and slowly replacing the brokenness of the multigenerational gang lifestyle.

Recently, The Center held a special event that showcased God's influence: the wedding of Ernesto "Daniel" and Becca De LaRosa, two community members who met in 1997 as elementary students at The Center. Bob Margaron, director of The Center, fondly remembers Becca running up to him one day with tears streaming down her cheeks, saying, "Daniel won't quit picking on me." Knowing this to be uncharacteristic for Daniel, who was generally quiet and gentle-spirited, Bob asked, "Do you think he likes you?" Becca ran away, yelling, "Eww!" Little could anyone predict how Bob's comment would foreshadow future events.

Both Daniel and Becca came from broken households, and each family knew hardship and heartache well. Daniel grew up in a single parent home, and Becca's father was incarcerated for much of her childhood. Becca married a man in the Marine Corps and become a mother of two but left her husband and returned to Stockton after he became abusive.

Daniel had remained unmarried and was working steadily. When Becca returned, they reconnected and moved in together. He embraced her two children as his own, and together they had a baby.

As their household grew, God moved in Daniel and Becca's hearts, burdening them with the desire to honor Him by being married. They sought Bob out. He agreed to officiate the wedding and walked with them through premarital counseling for three months. The couple also agreed to abstain from sex until they were married legally.

Becca dreamed of marrying Daniel in the place where they'd met, so the Margarons joyfully opened The Center's facilities for the wedding. The De LaRosas have been a testimony in Stockton. Together, they stood in front of the kids at The Center and spoke about their experience.

At the wedding, friends and family witnessed their passion for glorifying God as they stepped away from sin and into His design for their lives.

16

TELL IT TO THE NATIONS

STAN TOLER

*"Day after day, in the temple courts and from house to
house, they never stopped teaching and proclaiming the
good news that Jesus is the Messiah."*
– Acts 5:42

Christ-followers are not called to covert opera-
tions. Jesus intended for the world to "break our
cover." The mission of the disciples underscores it: "Jesus
himself sent them out from east to west with the sacred
and unfailing message of salvation that gives eternal life"
(Mark 16:8 NLT).

First-century Christians were tireless in their ministry.
They faced misunderstandings and misuse, but it only fu-

eled their fire. Their message and mission were powered by the Holy Spirit, setting the bar for all of us.

God sees you as a vital link in an ever-expanding mission: local, regional, and global.

Your story began with your faith in the Lord Jesus Christ as your Savior. You live out that story on the streets of your life. And you defend it by your knowledge of biblical beliefs. Then, you share your story. Why? Because someone may be lost if they don't hear it.

New Testament Christians (Acts 5:42) give you a strategy:

- Make sharing your story a daily goal - "day by day."

- Use every opportunity to share your story - "in the temple...house to house."

- Include your story in your conversations - "they never stopped teaching and proclaiming."

- Talk more about Jesus than yourself in your story - "the good news that Jesus is the Messiah."

"*We've a story to tell to the nations,*" and for you, that task begins right where you are. Who is the person you will reach with the good news today?

THINK ABOUT THIS

"God forbid that I should travel with anybody a quarter of an hour without speaking of Christ to them."
– George Whitefield

MY PRAYER

Lord, thank you for my story. Empower me to share it everywhere. Even today. Amen.

TRY IT

Be alert for a divine appointment today.

STORIES OF TRANSFORMATION

If You Will Help Me

Frank Martin | Retired Support Staff

The *Call, July/August/September 2017*

I grew up in a Christian home and went to church from the time I was born. Around the age of 12, I attended my first youth camp, where I came to understand who Christ Jesus truly is and committed my life to Him. After I graduated from high school, I went to camp one more time before heading off to my first year of college. It was during that camp that I felt the call to Christian ministry.

For sure, I didn't know what that meant. Was it to be a pastor, a missionary, a Christian teacher, or what? I just knew in my heart that the Lord wanted me to serve in a fulltime capacity.

When I returned home, I didn't have a pastor to talk to about this call. Our church was between pastors and the laymen were holding it together until one could be found. It was during this in-between time that I had a long talk with the Lord, asking Him just what it was He wanted me to do.

I can take you to the very spot in our backyard where this conversation took place. We had a little bridge over the sulfur creek that ran along the back of our property. I took out my Bible and asked the Lord what He wanted me to do.

Now I need to let you know that I'm not one of those people who opens the Bible up and then drops a finger on a verse to find direction. But what I did see as I studied the gospels was that Jesus used parables to get His message across. A parable is an earthly story with a heavenly principle.

I told the Lord that if He would help me with stories and object lessons like He used, then I would speak for Him. There was no lightning in the sky or thunder. There was no warm and fuzzy feeling in my chest. There was no tap on my shoulder by an angel. I just poured out my heart, and He listened.

From that point on, I noticed that I could remember stories and jokes easily. Then the object lessons started coming. I hardly ever speak without something in my hand to show the audience. When I see their eyes shine with understanding, I know they got the point!

I started speaking at the age of 18. Now I've just retired. And guess what? The Lord is still giving me object lessons and stories to use for Him! How cool is that? And I'm still saying, "if He will help me, I will."

17

THE LORD DELIVERS

DAN SCHAFER

"Seek his will in all you do, and he will
show you which path to take."
— Proverbs 3:6 NLT

We followed proper procedure, so the outcome should have been different.

We wanted to drive over Mt. Hood to explore its beauty, but it was raining. We were in Oregon for only a couple of days, so it was now or never. As we started out toward Mt. Hood in the borrowed car of a friend, it was a sunny day. It had only started raining as we neared the mountain. Having lived in California for a couple of years, we knew that rain in the valley could easily mean snow in the mountains. And so, we did the reasonable, practical thing – we stopped at the ranger's station at the base of the mountain, told him our plans, and asked whether the weather would be a problem.

"No. You should be fine," he responded. "It is snowing up top, but only down to around the 8,000-foot level. The passes are at 6,000 feet, so you should be able to drive up and over with no problem. The decision was made, and we began the climb. As we neared the first pass, the rain drops suddenly began to take shape on our car window. Time to turn around.

As I maneuvered to change direction, I spotted a car in the ditch, and continued to his location. Just then a tow truck pulled up from the direction we were wanting to travel. Having been assured everyone was okay in the car, I asked the driver of the tow truck, how the roads were ahead. "Absolutely, fine." And so, again assured that it was reasonable to continue, we set out to complete our journey over the mountain.

As we cleared the pass, we started on a long downward section of the road. The snow began falling at a rate I have never experienced any time before or since in my life. Now was not a good time to recall that my friend had told me the tires on his car were in need of replacement. The next 45-minutes found my wife and I both hanging out the windows of the car. She on the passenger side trying to see the edge of the road on the right, and I on the driver's side trying to see the edge of the road on the left.

We have never been as glad than when we finally arrived in the little town of Government Camp. We found a hotel and spent the night as the snow continued to fall – 18 inches worth by morning.

I sought the LORD, and he answered me; he delivered me from all my fears. Psalm 34:4

THINK ABOUT THIS

"The wise man in the storm prays to God, not for safety from danger, but for the deliverance from fear. It is the storm within that endangers him, not the storm without."
– Ralph Waldo Emerson

MY PRAYER

Lord, we need Your deliverance. Whether from trials that seem trivial, or from things or people that threaten our lives. In each case, we need deliverance from fear, so that we can find your hand of guidance. Amen.

TRY IT

Ask 3 people to describe something that God has delivered them from.

STORIES OF TRANSFORMATION

Escaping Home
Adhanom Hidug | Missionary, South Sudan

The Call, *July/August/September 2016*

Nine years ago, my friend and I had to escape from a political system that not only wanted to stop us from practicing the Christian faith, but also resolved to put us in prison because we followed Jesus. We walked for four days and three nights to enter a Sudanese border city. It was a very risky journey. The Eritrean border patrol units crisscross the terrain near the Sudanese border, and they have a "shoot to kill or injure" order against anyone leaving the country illegally. If we were to try to leave the country legally, it would be like a rat teasing a cat in an open field where it cannot hide.

God allowed us to walk through the camp of these units unnoticed. I wondered if He had made us invisible to them. We crossed a dry river without being physically aware of it. We only realized that it was a river bed after finding ourselves on the other side. God had changed the route we had planned to follow and made us follow a route He had planned for us.

As we slept for three nights in the open, He protected us from all sorts of fierce wild animals and helped us survive the extreme heat. He was in charge of our lives. Throughout the journey, I believed the words: "See, I am sending an angel ahead of you to guard you along the way and to bring you to the place I have prepared" as if they were said to me (Exodus 23:20).

I kept remembering Jesus, who had to escape to Egypt as a baby. I would pray, "Jesus, You made a risky journey while You were a baby. Please keep me safe."

While I was living with my family as a refugee in Kenya, I would pray, "Jesus, You once were a refugee in Egypt, and we are now refugees. Please, take care of us."

As refugees we had many challenges, but our main challenge was harassment and extortion by the police. However, the challenges only strengthened our faith in the Lord.

Now that I am in my newly adopted home among the friendly people of Edmonton, Alberta, Canada, I consider it a noble act and a ministry to regularly pray for Eritreans, Syrians, and people of other nationalities who are going through similar circumstances I went through.

The Lord delivers.

18

A GLOBAL HEART

STAN TOLER

*"God has chosen to make known among the
Gentiles the glorious riches of this mystery, which is
Christ in you, the hope of glory."*
– Colossians 1:27

John 3:16 might be called the key verse of the church:
"For God so loved the world that he gave his one
and only Son, that whoever believes in him shall not perish
but have eternal life." It is the personal focus for "whoever
believes."

Oh, how our hearts are stirred that those closest to us
may accept and act upon the truth of this Scripture. But
it also sparks a concern for those farthest away from us.

We are called to action in both settings. God sees us as appointed missionaries to the mission field of the home, but also to the community and to the world.

The scope of our concern for the lost must cover the width of the world, not just the walls of our home or the borders of our community. Local missions is our immediate context, but our responsibility is far wider. John the apostle reminds us of Christ's mission: "He is the atoning sacrifice for our sins, and not only for ours but also for the sins of the whole world" (1 John. 2:2).

The heart of Christ reaches us in our personal and local interests, but we can't afford to forget that it reaches to those anywhere and everywhere.

THINK ABOUT THIS
"World missions was on God's mind from the beginning."
– Dave Davidson

MY PRAYER
Stir my heart, O Lord, for those nearest me and for those farthest away. Amen.

TRY IT
Adopt a "sister city" approach to missions by choosing one international city to pray for daily, in addition to your own.

STORIES OF TRANSFORMATION

Open Arms
Kristen Tropf | Volunteer, Spain

The Call, *July/August/September 2016*

It's said you never truly understand someone until you walk a mile in their shoes. I never imagined I'd experience life as an immigrant, but several years ago God led me to live in a foreign country to work with immigrants. An immigrant living alongside immigrants.

I didn't expect it to be easy living in a foreign country, but it was much harder than I expected. Between language learning, government paperwork, culture shock, learning how to do simple tasks in a different context, and being far from family, sometimes just getting through the day was a victory!

As I adjusted to life in a foreign country and got to know my students and listen to their stories, I got a closeup view of their difficulties. Many came here in search of a better life or more opportunities but have only been disappointed with the outcome. Others feel alone and isolated—far away from loved ones and at odds with the new culture.

At times they feel unaccepted and unwelcome in this new land. It's here in this vulnerable state, far from all that is familiar, that God gives us the precious opportunity to be Jesus in the flesh to them. We have the privilege to show His acceptance, love, and grace. We can welcome them with open arms.

God has always had a soft spot in His heart for the marginalized—the foreigner, the widow, the orphan, the poor. He longs for us, His redeemed people, to also share His heart of compassion. Here are a few practical suggestions for ways we can reach out to immigrants or those new to our country:

- Invite someone from another country to your home for a meal.

- Offer to practice English conversation with them.

- Learn about their culture and worldview—they have rich experiences to share.

- Assist with healthcare processes or enrolling children in school.

May we remember that we also are foreigners here, awaiting our permanent home, our true country. And then may we bring a part of that Kingdom here to earth by loving those who are far from their home.

19

WE ARE THE INTERFACE

STAN TOLER

"I urge you, brothers and sisters, in view of God's mercy, to offer your bodies as a living sacrifice."
— Romans 12:1

Merriam-Webster's dictionary describes "Interface" as "the place at which independent and often unrelated systems meet and act on or communicate with each other."

Imagine that you had never heard the message of the gospel. Then imagine how you would react in some typical Christian contexts. Your first church service. Your first Bible reading. Your first religious song. It would seem mysterious. Now think about the first time someone explained the gospel to you or think about the testimony of that believer who sparked your interest in knowing more about Jesus.

Someone humorously suggested that a church without glass doors is like a tavern with its windows covered. While we wouldn't agree with linking the two, the principle is interesting. Those who have never visited a church might have that same sense of mystery as those who have never been to a tavern.

Paul the apostle gave his life in taking the *mystery* out of the *message.* His delighted in opening doors and removing coverings to let people know the glorious simplicity of the gospel. Those who were left out had been brought in. Those who were ignorant about biblical truth were now enlightened.

We are the interface. We are the connection between the known and unknown. Christ the Messiah has come to bring the hope of glory to the despised and despairing of earth. God sees you as someone on whom He depends to tell others how He can bring heaven's riches into the hearts of earth's impoverished—one person at a time.

THINK ABOUT THIS

"As long as there are millions destitute of the
Word of God and knowledge of Jesus Christ,
it will be impossible for me to devote time and
energy to those who have both."

– J. L. Ewen

MY PRAYER

Lord, use me as the connection to your wonderful message today. Show me one opportunity to make the message plain to someone who needs to know. Amen.

TRY IT

On an index card, write the gospel message using words that any unchurched person could understand.

STORIES OF TRANSFORMATION

The Adventure of Altar Living
Amanda Hoogkamp/ Missionary, Bolivia

The Call, *July/August/September 2017*

"It's a dangerous business, Frodo, going out your door. You step onto the road, and if you don't keep your feet, there's no knowing where you might be swept off to."

This quote from J. R. R. Tolkien in *The Fellowship of the Ring* reminds me of what it means to put your life on God's altar. There isn't any knowing what God is going to use or when; He often takes a piece of my life and uses it in ways that I never could have dreamed.

One of these instances was during my first two years in Bolivia. I felt God calling me to Bolivia to work with the El Alfarero (The Potter) University Student Center as a counselor. However, I could not start counseling right away because I needed to understand the language and culture better, so I volunteered wherever I could.

I began working in the café that served the students; making coffees and smoothies and serving food was my day-to-day ministry. It was an adventure. I had never worked in anything like that before. (I didn't even like coffee at the time; although, that is a different story now!)

Then they asked if I could help in the onsite library that was used by students, counselors, and the public. Sure, I thought; I love books. As I started working, I realized that maybe God had a different plan. You see, I not only love books, I also love libraries.

My family had a personal library in our house, and my mom had worked in a library for many years. I used to go in and help her with cataloging and shelving. It turned out that I knew more about running a library than most of those who were working in this library.

By the second year, I was working on updating the library and dealing with issues that had been there since it first opened. God took my life experiences—ones I never thought would be used on the field—and swept them up into His plans.

I had placed my life and experiences on His altar, and He took off what He wanted to use.

20

ABUNDANTLY BEYOND

DAN SCHAFER

"I became a servant of this gospel by the gift of God's
grace given me through the working of his power."
– Ephesians 3:7

In that moment, it seemed as though my heart had stopped. The surgeon stepped out of the operating room to inform me about the outcome of my wife's surgery. Just three days earlier, he had told us that she desperately needed surgery as bile was leaking into her abdominal cavity due to an earlier botched surgery. "Unfortunately," he continued, I can't operate at this time. If I operated now, she wouldn't make it because her body is too weak from the major infection she got in the ICU after her previous surgery."

Two days later, the surgery was back on; his message, even more sobering. "I have to operate now, because she is getting worse, not better."

We both knew what this meant. Unable to survive surgery earlier, she may not make it, now that she was two days worse. And so, just prior to her being wheeled off to the operating room, we said our goodbyes to each other.

I thought I was prepared for the surgeon's pronouncement as he came out of the operating room. But the reality is, I wasn't. His words were a major shock. "She made it!" I couldn't believe my ears. She had survived. God had performed a miracle!

"Now to Him who is able to do far more abundantly beyond all that we ask or think, according to the power that works within us, to Him be the glory in the church and in Christ Jesus to all generations forever and ever. Amen" (Ephesians 3:20). My wife's ordeal was a very lengthy, and tiring experience. When she was taken away to surgery, I was resigned to the fact she might die. But literally, thousands of people all around the world were praying for my wife.

My faith had not been great enough to believe that God was going to touch her; but God is able to do far more than we even ask or think – abundantly beyond *all* that we ask or think. In those moments, without even knowing it, I had borrowed the faith of a thousand other Christians.

It is true, we ask God for a lot. It is equally true that God is able to do abundantly beyond all that we ask or think. His resources? The power that works within us – His power. The full resources of the One who created the universe are at work for you. No, the Scriptures makes it even more personal than that: Those resources *are* working in you.

THINK ABOUT THIS
"Can you think of anything in your
life that is big to God?"
– G. Campbell Morgan

MY PRAYER
Lord, when we don't have sufficient faith to see Your provision, help us to borrow the faith of all those who are praying for us. Amen.

TRY IT
"Loan" your faith to someone who is discouraged and pray for them what they can't pray for themselves.

STORIES OF TRANSFORMATION

Not One Has Been Lost

Joanna Coppedge | Missionary, Uganda

The Call, *July/August/September 2016*

The beauty of the gospel is that it doesn't matter where we are from, where we currently call home, or where our passport leans heavy on stamps. Jesus loves us all and came to make His home in us, if we will but welcome Him!

After having recently given birth to our fifth baby on our *third* continent, I am beginning to wonder if I might need to look more closely at this issue of migration and the loss of one's home and home culture. And with our family growing, it is no longer just my husband and I who must answer these questions of cultural identity.

Our children still consider their home in Arua, Uganda, to be their true home. One is certain that she is from the United States of America (where we have never lived as a family, only visited, but it is our passport country and grandparents' home).

Another asks when we go to the grocery store if we are going to Scotland now, or if we are still in St. Andrews (we currently live in St. Andrews, Scotland).

And our youngest is currently waiting for his residence visa...some claim so he can legally be in our family!

Needless to say, we have some culturally confusing conversations around our breakfast table. 1 Peter 1:1-2 (MSG) talks of exiles: "I, Peter, am an apostle on assignment by Jesus, the Messiah, writing to exiles scattered to the four winds. Not one is missing, not one forgotten. God the Father has his eye on each of you, and has determined by the work of the Spirit to keep you obedient through the sacrifice of Jesus. May everything good from God be yours!"

As I recently prepared a Bible study on this text and prayed over it, it brought me continually to my children, and their own apparent rootlessness. Will they grow and be just scattered, blowing in the wind? It was quite a frightening thought.

The Father patiently encouraged me to read on: "Not one is missing, not one forgotten." His attention is on each one of them. He knows them by name and has good, pleasing, and perfect plans for them. Jesus Himself has redeemed them, and they are kept by His Holy Spirit.

These promises provide security and hope for a wanderer in this world. What confidence we can have even when our passport is thick and growing. He sees us, knows us, and keeps us.

In fact, the company of wanderers is not all bad. The call of Abram to leave his own country and walk with God has had a profound effect on my own walking out of my faith and following Jesus. Abraham's migrating and leaving of family and home culture ultimately proved to be a significant part of God's redemptive plan for the globe.

We are witnessing a great migration here in Europe today. Horrible atrocities are forcing millions from their homes. Yet, spiritual persecution, mass exodus, and homelessness are not new or unique to this day and age. Such struggles and transitions are as old as Genesis. Just as Abram had to choose to trust God on his wandering journey, so also am I learning to trust Him. Even more, I am learning to trust Him with my family.

Will you pray with us for those on unplanned migrations around the world, seeking stability, that they will seek Jesus?

21

STAYING ON-MESSAGE

STAN TOLER

*"Continue in what you have learned and have
become convinced of, because you know those
from whom you learned it."*
– 2 Timothy 3:14

John Wesley said, "I want the whole Christ for my Savior, the whole Bible for my book, the whole Church for my fellowship, and the whole world for my mission field."

What a dynamic vision! And that vision was connected to a dynamic message of saving and sanctifying faith in Christ, and Holy Spirit power to live and serve victoriously in the world. Both his vision and his message have endured through the ages.

Vision must always have a message to be effective. And that message must always be firmly planted in the Word of God. "On message" means that our words align with the kingdom and the Word.

The content of our message is always important, and the way it is shared can add to its impact.

- Keep it simple. The average person reads at about a seventh-grade level. That, and a great biblical illiteracy problem, makes it important to simplify the gospel message—without dumbing it down.

- Saturate it with prayer. The Holy Spirit promised to empower our gospel message. One to one, or one to a crowd, pray that the Spirit will link biblical truth to the listener.

- Accompany it with kindness. You earn a listen by the way you treat the listener. Christlikeness makes sharing the truth transformational.

Your life in Christ is the greatest proof that your message works. God sees you as a powerful communicator. And He promises to add His power to the message you will share.

THINK ABOUT THIS

"What an incredible witness it is to a lost and fearful society when the Christian acts like a child of God, living under the loving sovereignty of the Heavenly Father."
– Henry Blackaby

MY PRAYER

Lord, thank You for letting me share the greatest message the world will ever hear. I am relying on you for insight and opportunity to do that well today. Amen.

TRY IT

Today, strike up a conversation with an unchurched person, and begin by listening.

STORIES OF TRANSFORMATION

Outsiders on the Inside

Rachel Elwood | Staff Writer with Mark and Kim
| Volunteers, North America

The Call, *July/August/September 2016*

"God is doing something big with Chinese people." Six years ago, Mark and Kim began attending a Chinese church. But that was just one step in their journey to reaching out to Chinese immigrants and students. They served at Tenwek Hospital in Kenya for seven years. Prior to that, they had gone on several international medical short-term trips and helped revitalize an inner-city church.

When God led them to return to the United States, they were uncertain what the next step would be. They attended a CMDA (Christian Medical and Dental Associations) conference and were told by an acquaintance, "You need to work with the Chinese." Two years of exploring, or "floundering," according to Mark, followed.

Mark and Kim began attending the Chinese church and, step by step, became involved in various ways. They have worked with the youth group, taught parenting classes, and led outreach to university students. Mark is a deacon, and Kim is on the missions committee.

Doors have also opened that have taken them to China to work with medical outreach. Still, it took time—almost a year—to build relationships and gain a better understanding of the community. "Because of our experience as cross-cultural workers, we were comfortable being outsiders," Kim said. "We were prepared to listen, to learn, and to be in it for the long haul."

That willingness to stick with it earned them the respect of the community, which was further deepened when they went to China for the first time. Mark and Kim have learned many things during their years of involvement in the Chinese community. Here are a few of their takeaways that might be helpful to you as you reach out to internationals in your town.

1. Look around you. Who is lonely? Who is international? Look for opportunities to reach out to immigrants. Be aware of special holidays. Chinese New Year is a big deal for those Mark and Kim work with but consider Eid or Cinco de Mayo. Invite people to your house or invite them to share their ethnic foods. "Most university students who come here to study will never set foot into an American home. Look for ways to reach out!" suggested Kim.

2. Don't worry about being an expert in the culture or about not having all the answers to every spiritual question. "It's freeing to realize we don't have all the answers," Mark said. "But the Bible does have the answers we seek. We can study together to find them."

3. When joining a more established church or ministry, be willing to be a part of what is going on, not trying to change them to be like "us." Kim shared that when she joined her church's missions committee, she waited a full year before making any suggestions.

4. Welcome newcomers to this country by offering practical help. "Regardless of culture, most people appreciate a genuine outreach of friendship," said Mark.

5. Listen. "Everyone has a story, and theirs might be more interesting than yours," emphasized Kim. Most importantly, realize that God is sovereign and will guide your steps. Mark shared that if they had gotten involved with the Chinese church earlier, during their two years of searching, it might not have worked well because of other circumstances at the church. "Sometimes God makes you flounder," Mark said. "But it's always for a reason."

These advance volunteers look forward to what God has in store for their future outreach to Chinese people, both in the United States and in China.

22

YOU ARE THE MESSENGER

STAN TOLER

*"Be on your guard; stand firm in the faith; be cou-
rageous; be strong. Do everything in love."*
— 1 Corinthians 16:13–14

Who gave you the gospel? That person, at that time, in that setting, made an everlasting dif-ference in your life. The personal faithfulness of that wit-ness was the audiovisual that communicated the truth of their gospel.

Paul gave two important messages to his spiritual son, Timothy. First, you are a debtor. "From whom you learned," someone lived and preached God's Word in such a way that it impacted your life. For Timothy, the seeds of Christian service were sown by godly family members and committed disciples. Their message became his.

Second, you are a messenger, "continue in what you have learned." The baton has been passed, and the next lap is yours. The Old Testament examples of Elijah passing the leadership "uniform" to Elisha, or Moses turning the "game plan" over to Joshua, are just two of numerous incidents where the faithfulness of one servant influenced the service of another.

In many nations or communities, the gospel message will be covered by the message of humanism unless a messenger is faithful to the Word and his or her calling. That scenario brings additional needs to mind: the need for a spiritual and ministerial faithfulness of current messengers, and the need for more messengers.

You and I stand in the gap. We are the messenger, gifted with God's Word, and called to find, train, and send other messengers.

THINK ABOUT THIS
"Spreading the gospel isn't solely the church's job;
it's the job of every Christian."
– Paul Chappell

MY PRAYER
Jesus, the baton of your Word is in my hands. Give me strength to run the race, and wisdom to pass the baton to another. Amen.

TRY IT
Encourage a younger Christian today.

STORIES OF TRANSFORMATION

Where Brokenness Abounds
Betsy Tejeda | Missionary, Texas/Mexico Border Ministries

The Call, *October/November/December 2016*

As a missionary in McAllen, Texas, these are just a few of the heart-wrenching stories of the people in our community.

- A single mother, terrified she's pregnant again, is already being pushed by the father to get an abortion.

- A teenager, so drugged up with his friends, can barely remember what happened one night.

- A 23-year-old mother of six, evicted from a tiny one-room apartment because her husband made the choice to try cocaine and got thrown in jail, has no way to pay the rent.

- A woman, sobbing, deals with the fact that her oldest son is involved in drugs and gangs.

- A man, so overwrought from losing his job and not being able to support his family, turns to alcohol.

- A teenage girl, holding on to a secret she should never have been told, struggles in her relationship with her parents.

The needs are overwhelming, and the amount of brokenness that abounds is astonishing. What can we do? How can we help? Is there a way to help them pick up the pieces of their lives?

For a brief moment, it's tempting to have a "ride in and save the day" mentality. But, the truth is quickly clear. We cannot be their savior. Although there are many ways we can serve this community, the problems they encounter are God-sized.

The reality is that no amount of money, counseling, clothing, or food can really repair the damage done and fix the underlying issue: SIN.

Our only hope is to point them to the true Savior. Share with them about the One who can forgive their sins and give them a second chance. Direct them to the Redeemer who will give them a new beginning, even as they face the consequences of their sin. Show them love: all-encompassing, all-fulfilling, all-enveloping love. Steer them to hope, and remind them that they are loved, seen, and valued.

As I listen to their stories, I am reminded it is my story, also. I, too, came to a place of brokenness, realizing I needed a Savior. My choices were different. My consequences may not have been as public, but I needed forgiveness and a new start. Now I pray my life is a testimony to these dear ones so that they, too, can be forgiven and healed, filled with hope, and joyful in a promising future.

In the midst of their brokenness, may give them hope by pointing them to the Savior.

23

THE GREAT COMBINATION

STAN TOLER

*"Oh, my dear children! I feel as if I'm going through
labor pains for you again, and they will continue
until Christ is fully developed in your lives."*
— Galatians 4:19 NLT

The Great Commission tells us what to do: make disciples of all nations. The Great Commandment tells us how to do it: while loving God with all our hearts, and loving others as ourselves. The "Great Combination" would have us minister to the nations with hearts filled with the love of God.

The cross covers both the unlovely and the lovely. It makes no distinction based on race, class, or ideology. Jesus is the equal opportunity Savior, dying for everyone, everywhere, to give them an equal freedom from their past and a hope for their future.

The very heart of the child of God is filled with the love of God—it has been "shed abroad in our heart" (Romans 5:5 KJV). But the child of God fully surrendered to Him is not only filled with His love but also *controlled* by His love. Every minister, at home or overseas, must come to the decision that God is in control of the past, present, and future of their life and work.

World Vision founder Bob Pierce once said, "Let my heart be broken with the things that break God's heart." To picture Jesus overlooking Jerusalem with a broken heart over the need of its citizens and his longing to meet it is to know what breaks God's heart.

But a heart broken for others must first be broken of self. The gospel song *Search Me, O God* has these words, "Lord, take my life, and make it wholly Thine; fill my poor heart with Thy great love divine." A missional and transformational love for the lost comes from the heart that is controlled by God's love.

God sees you as a beloved child who inwardly longs to be more like their loving Heavenly Father.

THINK ABOUT THIS

"I continue to dream and pray about a revival
of holiness in our day that moves forth in mission
and creates authentic community."
– John Wesley

MY PRAYER

Lord, I gratefully surrender all that I know of myself
to all that I know of you. Let me be filled with your Spirit,
and ready to do your work. Amen.

TRY IT

As you go about your day today, observe others and try
to see them as Jesus does.

STORIES OF TRANSFORMATION

Living in Community
Dora Wesche | Retired Missionary, Kenya

The Call, *October/November/December 2016*

"May the God who gives endurance and encouragement give you the same attitude of mind toward each other that Christ Jesus had" (Romans 15:5).

Sometimes it takes a heaping measure of grace to live on a foreign mission station. I didn't get the hang of it in the beginning, but failure can be the back door to success.

My husband, Bob, our one-year-old daughter, Dawn, and I first arrived in Kenya in 1967. As we faced challenges, some memories stand out, specifically in areas of obeying authority, loving your neighbor, and "keeping up with the Joneses."

One day, Bob had come home from a long day at the hospital, and I was giving vent to a list of frustrations. As I paused for a breath, Bob, known for his one-liners, said, "You are saying you know how to run the mission better than the mission leaders." Totally shocked, I thought it over. I was even more shocked to realize it was true—not that I could run things better than the leaders but that I thought I could.

A new missionary had arrived on the field. His ideas were different, feathers were ruffled, and there were some unflattering comments made. During a chapel service at a retreat, this strong impression came to mind: "Do you want him to accept you just as you are, with all your faults?" Well, yes; I hadn't thought about that before. "Then accept him just as he is with all of his faults." I applied that lesson many times in the years that followed.

One day, the door flew open; our little toddler spread her hands out wide and in great frustration asked, "WHERE is my little red wagon?" Oh! We had brought dolls and lots of games but NO red wagon. However, since a neighbor's child had one, Dawn wanted one, too! We all needed to learn about finding contentment in what we had.

I learned to thank God that I didn't have to worry about running the mission, and I marveled at leaders who were exercising their gifts of administration, of which I have none.

Today, some of my dearest friends are "old" retired missionaries as well as wonderful new "young" missionaries on the field. I am eternally grateful that God brought us together. I am also coming closer to learning to be content in all things.

Being a missionary brought the greatest joys of my life. I love The One who taught me how.

24

DON'T WORRY; BE HAPPY!

DAN SCHAFER

"Cast all your anxiety on him
because he cares for you."
— 1 Peter 5:7

Despite my best efforts to keep it at bay, fear crept into my heart. It was a cold, wet night as my wife and I carefully ascended the metal stairway. I ducked as I entered the long narrow cylinder crowded with a hundred plus other passengers bound for Moscow.

We were scheduled to fly out of Kiev into these ominous dark skies in what appeared to be a very old plane operated by Aeroflot Airlines. As I took my seat, my comfort level fell even further as I examined the duct tape holding the interior panels in place and discovered that my seat no longer was capable of remaining in the "upright and locked position."

My mind couldn't help but play out a scenario where I told my wife how much I loved her as we plummeted out of the skies towards a remote wooded mountain side. Obviously, since I am currently writing these words, those fears never translated into reality.

It has been said that 95% of the things we worry about never happen. But that doesn't stop us from worrying. Worry is a powerful emotion that can paralyze us and render us useless for kingdom service.

This is why the Apostle Paul's advice to Christians is so vital, "Don't worry about anything; instead, pray about everything. Tell God what you need, and thank him for all he has done" (Phillippians 4:6). There is a principle to follow here. Worrying should be replaced by prayer.

Practically speaking, it is easier to stop something when you replace it with something else. It's hard to keep on worrying when your mind and heart are flooded with prayer. Prayer forces out the worry that has taken up residence in us. When we pray, there simply is no room remaining in us for worry.

Jesus also stressed this with one of His parables. "Now He was telling them a parable to show that at all times they ought to pray and not to lose heart" (Luke 18:1). Without prayer, worries take over; fears loom over us and rob us of our courage. Despair conquers us as we are wearied out and exhausted by our worries.

So, take Paul's advice and replace those worries with prayer. Tell God what you need and thank him for what he has done.

THINK ABOUT THIS

"Is prayer your steering wheel or your spare tire?"

– Corrie ten Boom

MY PRAYER

Lord, life gives me a lot to worry about. Please help me to remember that you have taught us not to allow those worries to persist, but to instead take our concerns to you in prayer. Amen.

TRY IT

Name three things that you worry about, and then practice praying for them right now.

STORIES OF TRANSFORMATION

An Unexpected Gift

Susana (Bev) Donahue | Missionary, Paraguay

The Call, *October/November/December 2016*

It would not be found on the list of Top 10 appropriate gifts to give a man. In fact, it would most likely show up on a list of gift suggestions for a new mother and her baby.

We were in Santa Cruz, Bolivia, visiting some friends from our years in ministry there. I always try to stop by and greet my former hairdresser. This year, knowing that she and her husband would want to see our son, Andrés, too, the whole family paid a visit to her beauty salon. After we spent some time with her and her husband, she presented us each with small gifts. My gift was lotion, but Mark and Andrés both received a bottle of Johnson's baby powder. We graciously said, "thank you" (what else could we say?!) and went on our way.

Back home in Paraguay, it was a hot, hot summer. Some people do well with the heat while others suffer with uncomfortable heat rashes. Such was the case one evening when Mark encountered our neighbor, standing behind his wall with no shirt on, looking miserable with a heat rash. Mark soon learned that our neighbor had been exposed to too much sun and was suffering its effects. The neighbor said that he needed some Johnson's baby powder for his rash but that he did not have "ningún peso"—not one cent—to purchase it.

Seeing the need and hearing "Johnson's baby powder," Mark was alerted by the Holy Spirit that he could be a part of the solution. Mark promptly retrieved an unopened bottle of the baby powder. After Mark placed it in the neighbor's hands, the neighbor asked, "Is this a gift for me?" With a rejoicing heart, Mark affirmed that it was and watched a big smile spread across the man's face.

A gift from our friend in Bolivia is impacting our new community in Paraguay! God provided just what was needed. We pray that God will show us how to help our neighbor see a greater need in his life. We so desire that he sees his need to know our Jesus.

Sometimes we must see ways to help meet temporal needs before we have the privilege to speak to the greater need. How does God want to use you today? It may be to pass along an unexpected gift to someone in your community that needs it now. Don't miss the blessing!

25

GOOD GIFTS

DAN SCHAFER

"Now eagerly desire the greater gifts."
— 1 Corinthians 12:31

What had we gotten ourselves into? My wife and I arrived late in the evening at our accommodations. The thick darkness of our remote location didn't mask the strong barnyard odors as we approached the house. It was a penetrating stench that took our breath away.

With flashlights in hand, our good friend led us around to the other side of the structure - a traditional Swiss farmhouse, half house, half barn. Amazingly, once on the house side of the structure, we couldn't even get a hint of the odors that had overpowered us just moments earlier.

It was late, so we quickly settled into the bed. We were here for a long weekend arranged by our friend in the Swiss mountains. Just $20 per night. Our challenging beginning caused me to wonder if staying in this home might have been a mistake.

In the morning, I pulled back the curtains covering a large picture window in our bedroom. Once again, I felt breathless. I quickly implored my wife to join me at the window. We stood there in overwhelming excitement as we gazed out over the lushest green valley imaginable. It sloped down to a crystal-clear mountain creek that gave way to a majestic, towering snow cap mountain just beyond its banks. This live canvas was perfectly completed by an incredibly beautiful and inspiring waterfall coming down the mountain side.

We were further amazed later that day as something jumped out at us from the pages of a Swiss tourism magazine that we just happen to be thumbing through. There, on the two-page center photo in the middle of that high-resolution color image, was the very house in which we were staying.

Our significant apprehension was turned into total elation.

How often have we been too quick to judge our circumstances and express our dissatisfaction with God? God is leading us to His overwhelming beauty, but we only notice the pigpen on the way. In those moments, we are ready to turn around, and seek another path.

We need to remember that God delights in giving good gifts to His children. Jesus told His disciples, "If you then, being evil, know how to give good gifts to your children, how much more will your Father who is in heaven give what is good to those who ask Him!" (Matthew 7:11). Luke's version of this same conversation, adds one more important detail, making it clear that these good gifts include the giving of God's Holy Spirit to His children (Luke 11:13).

In Acts 19:2, when Paul came into Ephesus on one of his journeys and found some believers, he immediately questioned them, "Have you received the Holy Spirit since you have believed?" The splendor of this gift was paramount on Paul's mind when meeting Christians for the first time.

As you walk through this life, don't miss the beauty God has in store for you. Don't turn back because the terrain of consecration to His will gets rough, or the odor of self-surrender is unpleasant. Seek out God's good gift to you – the infilling of His Holy Spirit.

THINK ABOUT THIS

"Flee, then, to your atoning Savior,
who can forgive you, and welcome the Holy Spirit,
who can cleanse you."
– A.M. Hills

MY PRAYER

Lord, help me not to miss the gift of your Holy Spirit because of the difficult journey of self-surrender you require of me. Amen.

TRY IT

Name as many of God's "good gifts" to as you can in 60 seconds.

Stories of Transformation

Finding Community, Making Real Connections

Nathan Vitatoe | Volunteer, North America

The Call, *October/November/December 2016*

I walked through the door, and I was immediately met with the delicious aroma of good food lingering in the air. Bright tables and chairs were coupled with the familiar sound of rapid conversations in Spanish. I had stopped by a local Mexican restaurant to see if they would be interested in having me volunteer once a week to teach an English as a Second Language class before they opened for the day.

When my family and I first stepped back onto U.S. soil after serving North African immigrants in Spain for two years, I wasn't sure how God was going to use us for cross cultural ministry. However, we felt His presence and a peace about the decision to return and focus on bi-vocational ministry in WGM's Advance Volunteer Network.

The Lord has continued to expand our heart for the pilgrims of the world, this time in our own backyard of southern Ohio. There is a benefit to ministering to Spanish speakers in their own language, but many opportunities exist in communities all across our country in English.

One of the main lessons that the Lord has taught me through working with immigrants in Europe and the U.S. is that in order to build a relationship where we can share the hope we have in Jesus, the connections that we make have to be genuine. This valuable principle of authenticity in ministry has stuck with my wife, Kenzie, and me as we approach every new ministry opportunity.

Even as we began to plan for our mission trip to Spain, we utilized as a team the booklet, *Before You Pack Your Bag, Prepare Your Heart* by Cindy Judge, which was very helpful to us. As travelers of the gospel, we demonstrate our love for Spanish-speaking immigrants through genuine friendship and an interest in helping prepare them for day-to-day life.

Our Hispanic friends can feel isolated, both linguistically and culturally. The friendships that we have developed have opened doors to share the most important aspect of our lives, our faith and hope in Jesus Christ our Savior. Community isn't something we necessarily create; it's something that we find as we naturally connect with others. When the Holy Spirit urges us to share the love of Christ, we just need to take the step—without expecting anything in return.

26

GOD IS DOING A BIG THING

STAN TOLER

"I will make you into a great nation, and I will
bless you; I will make your name great, and you
will be a blessing. I will bless those who bless you,
and whoever curses you I will curse; and all peoples
on earth will be blessed through you."
— Genesis 12:2–3

God has always intended for His people to be the means through whom He would bless all nations. One of the reasons we are invited into His family is to take part in that mission. God sees you as means for blessing His world.

Most days that doesn't seem to be the case. Between trying to get bills paid, knock off a to-do list, and keep the family in order, it doesn't seem like our frenetic lives are much of a blessing to anyone. Like one dear saint put it, "The hurrier we go, the behinder we get!"

If you need to clearly see the big thing God is doing in the world and your part in it, consider this. Last year nearly 3 million people converted to Christianity. That number represents a city the size of Chicago. That many new souls entered the Kingdom, and you helped make it happen.

Christians are a blessing to their neighbors in nearly every place the church exists. The noted scholar Jürgen Habermas noted, "The individual morality of conscience, human rights and democracy, is the direct legacy of the Judaic ethic of justice and the Christian ethic of love."

The world is a better place because of the tireless ministry of countless Christ-followers just like you.

The American Hospital Association says there are 2,845 not-for-profit hospitals in the United States, many of which were started by Christian churches or ministries. The church is the largest single non-governmental provider of health care and education in the world.

And every day, you are a part of that great work. By making converts, discipling believers, training leaders, and, yes, knocking items off your to-do list, you are moving the mission of Jesus Christ forward in the world.

God sees you as a person who uses His wisdom and power in working for the kingdom in your community right now. You are part of the spiritual machinery He uses to do big things in His world.

THINK ABOUT IT

"Missions is the overflow of our delight in God, because missions is the overflow of God's delight in being God."
– John Piper

PRAYER

Lord, help me to see the big picture and know that I'm part of your plan. Amen.

TRY IT

Do an Internet search of world missions statistics.

STORIES OF TRANSFORMATION

Birdies for Babies

Pam Chupp | Former Missionary, Kenya

The Call, *October/November/December 2016*

Anna Redding came to Tenwek Hospital in 2014 with her father, Dr. Mark Redding. He is a neurosurgeon who was serving on his third short-term medical missions trip to Tenwek. When they returned home, Anna wondered if she could do something to make a difference in the lives of the babies and moms in Tenwek's nursery. She was entering her senior year of high school in North Carolina, and one of her senior assignments called for a community service project.

Anna and her dad thought and prayed about it, and Dr. Redding had an idea: "Anna, you love golf and are pretty good at it. Why not ask for people to pledge a gift for every birdie you make in your senior year golf season?" Anna looked carefully at her junior year performance and thought that for her senior year, she could possibly get three birdies per round. (A birdie is scoring one stroke under par per golf hole.)

She predicted that she might get 30 to 35 birdies that season. She went to work making phone calls and talking to friends at church, school, and in the community. They decided to call this project "Birdies for Babies."

Dr. Redding and Dr. David Hoover, president of *The Friends of Tenwek* organization, are friends, and Dr. Hoover suggested that this would be an exciting project for FOT. Pledges started coming in, and the fall high school girl's golf season began.

She played at a level that amazed her coach, teammates, and the competition. Averaging SIX birdies per round. Halfway through the season, Anna had already reached her prediction of 30 birdies. She asked her dad, "Should I stop, because we told the donors that I would drop around 30 birdies?

Mark and Anna decided she should push on and work harder, letting the donors decide what to do about their pledges. Every time she leaned over to sink a difficult putt, she thought about those tiny, premature babies in the Tenwek nursery.

By the end of the season, Anna had dropped 63 birdies and three eagles (scoring two under par) and was the number one female high school golfer in North Carolina! At the final tally, Anna had raised over $22,000 for the Tenwek nursery through "Birdies for Babies."

After consulting Tenwek pediatrician Dr. Chuck Bemm on the top need for the nursery, Anna and her father purchased a new GE Giraffe incubator. Anna and her father returned to Tenwek to see the incubator in use and found a tiny baby named Kipkoech Bett thriving inside. He was born prematurely, weighing only 1.65 pounds at birth.

In a dedication and appreciation ceremony, the nursery staff and members of the FOT Board gathered for prayer around the new incubator. My husband, Mike, read a letter to Anna.

Dear Anna,

We haven't been properly introduced yet, but we will forever be linked. My name is Kipkoech. I just woke up a few days ago. I was placed in a wooden box the day I was born because I needed help surviving this big world right now. I was given a new, shiny home. They told me that a very special girl came to Tenwek and fell in love with us little ones. Thank you, Anna Redding, for your love for Jesus.

Kipkoech

Placed in the Master's hand, a talent for putting a golf ball into the cup can make for a wonderful story like Anna's.

27

THE SEEKING GOD

STAN TOLER

"The Son of Man came to seek and to save the lost."
– Luke 19:10

Have you noticed it? The subtle inversion that's taken place in our thinking about our mission? Where once we focused our energies on the word, GO, we have now applied our thinking to strategies for getting nonbelievers to COME TO US. In the Gospels, God is pictured as the *seeker*, going into the world in search of lost sheep. Now, we imagine the lost person as the *seeker*, believing that unsaved people spend much of their energy asking, "Which church should I attend this weekend?"

Yet the Great Commission stands as written. It is a call—more than that, an imperative—to GO into the world and make disciples of all nations. Jesus Christ entered the world to be among those whom He would save. In that grand act, God drew near to the those far away.

Understanding the heart of God is the key to being mobilized for the mission. So long as we imagine God plaintively waiting for lost people to stumble upon the truth, we will never be inspired to go into all the world. But the moment we realize that God Himself is the seeker, scouring the highways and byways in search of "the least of these," we'll be compelled to go with Him.

When you seek to understand the heart of God, you will love as He loves and do as He does. So, when someone asks, "Do you personally know any seekers?" you can enthusiastically answer, "Yes, I do. And you're looking at one."

God sees you as a follower of His truth and grace who, out of love and obedience, seeks others.

THINK ABOUT THIS

"The Great Commission is not an option to be considered; it is a command to be obeyed."

– Hudson Taylor

MY PRAYER

Lord, rouse me from complacency and give me an urgency to do Your work. Amen.

TRY IT

List 5 people who would be open to your sharing Christ with them; pray every day over them; and take a step in reaching the first one on your list.

STORIES OF TRANSFORMATION

A Chaplain's Diary
Eliphas Mutegi | Chaplain, Kenya

The Call, *December 2017*

I accepted Jesus Christ as my personal Savior in 1976. From then on, I started witnessing about the love of Jesus Christ. After completing college, I continued doing the same within my home area. In the early 1990s, I started venturing farther. I was involved in nursing services and sharing the good news with the patients as a chairman of my church's missions committee. In March 2016, I became a full-time chaplain after completing theological training by extension.

I have seen God do many great things. Here are some of my favorite stories of God working in amazing ways. They are stories that prove, without a doubt, the truth of His Word.

- A Muslim man who was paralyzed and had contractures (permanently bent limbs or joints) became healed after many prayers. This was a miracle! Even greater, this man accepted Jesus as his Savior.

- A young university student was admitted who had gone mad and was hallucinating, saying he was God the Creator. He found deliverance after hearing God's Word, followed by a prayer of faith and subsequent counseling.

- A man with a severe heart problem called me when he was at the point of death. He told me that he was once a believer but had walked away from his faith. He wanted to repent and come back to Jesus. After prayers, God did another miracle; the man got better.

- A young boy had attempted suicide by taking poison. His relatives were distraught because of the deep coma he was in, and they couldn't afford medical treatment. I prayed for the family, and we were able to find help for them. Three days later, the boy had recovered and accepted Christ as his Savior.

- A girl who had been involved in devil worship was admitted with a fractured leg. After I realized this, I called her to the chapel. And after intensive prayer, Jesus delivered her. She told us her story about how her cousin who is a magician introduced her to devil worship. When she went back to the patient ward, other patients wondered at the change in her; she left with scary, wild eyes and came back filled with peace.

- During the last year, over 250 souls have been saved through our ministry.

This is God's doing. May He be glorified through all these miracles and transformations!

28

THE HIDDEN PURPOSE

DAN SCHAFER

"There is an appointed time for everything. And there is a time for every event under heaven."
— Ecclesiastes 3:1 NASB

My wife awoke in a panic as her body was suddenly jerked slightly forward. Upon opening her eyes from an unintentional nap in the car, she could see absolutely nothing through the front window. The jerk she had felt was the result of a quick tap I had instinctively made on the brakes. Without warning, we were racing into a snow squall at 70 mph – complete white out conditions.

I had a decision to make. If I stopped or slow down too quickly, we would be hit from behind. If I didn't slow down, we would hit others in front of us.

As I began to slow, I thought I saw an exit sign. I maneuvered toward it, and in moments we were able to safely escape the highway.

Conditions in life can change quickly and unexpectedly. An accident, a diagnosis, a firing, or a partner who announces they are no longer committed to a marriage. They all are examples of factors that can suddenly redirect our lives, even endanger them. While such events may bring panic to our lives, God never breaks a sweat. He knows the future, and He has it all under control. Romans 8:28 reminds us that "God causes all things to work together for good to those who love God, to those who are called according to His purpose."

Joseph experienced this when his brothers threw him into a pit. Murder filled their hearts until it was replaced with greed, selling their brother to strangers and into a life of slavery.

Surely, in that moment Joseph was in the depths of despair. As he was led away in chains, he likely watched his brothers head toward home, laughing in joy about their deceit and the good fortune that lined their pockets. They had ignored his desperate pleas, and he sensed only cruelty from his new companions.

He didn't understand then, what he would understand later. His brothers' actions were meant for evil, but God meant them for good (Genesis 50:20). God took their evil tactics and used them to execute a plan of protection for the lives of the entire family of Jacob, including not only Joseph, but all his brothers. A plan that would take many years to unfold.

God is still in the business of using man's evil intent to bring about the good of His plans. Trust His heart, and trust that He will cause your circumstances to work together for your good.

THINK ABOUT THIS
"God would never permit any evil if he could not bring good out of evil."
– Thomas Watson

MY PRAYER
Lord, help me to remember that You cause all things to work together for Your good, and not to become discouraged when others take actions toward me with evil intent. Amen.

TRY IT
List 3 times when you have seen God bring something good out of something bad.

STORIES OF TRANSFORMATION

The Power of Changed Lives
Debbie Cartwright | Missionary,
American Indian Field (Arizona)

The Call, *October/November/December 2016*

One changed life can make quite a difference in a community. Two changed lives? Even better!

There was a time when Mike and Delia weren't very good parents or very good citizens of their community. Their lives were wrapped up in their addictions. But Jesus changed that in a powerful way, thanks to the fervent prayers of Mike's mother and her church family.

Suddenly, Mike and Delia became the parents their children had needed for years. But, even more than that, they became surrogate parents to youth in the community who needed love and support. They brought children to church, fed them when they were hungry, and became attentive to their needs and prayer concerns.

However, one thing held them back; they had never been legally married. They hadn't been following Christ for very long when they sensed that this was something they had to make right. They could have quietly held a private ceremony with a few family members, but that wasn't the call they felt from God. No, their wedding was to be a witness to the community and an act of worship with their church family.

They asked for their vows to be completed as part of a Sunday morning church service. On that special day, we sang hymns together and prayed for the needs of the community. Then my husband, Steve's, weekly "sermon" was a Christian wedding ceremony, celebrating the commitment of these two people and their new lives in Christ.

The bride and groom made their promises to one another before the church family and many, many friends from their "old lives." Their wedding attendants and ring bearers were their own precious children, beaming with pride.

It was a powerful testimony that reached into many hearts. One young man came to Steve after the ceremony and said, with tears in his eyes, "I can't get over the change in their lives. If God can do this for them, do you think He can do this for me?" He received the assurance that God's mighty power could work in his life, too. There at the wedding, he prayed for Christ to change his heart and life. What an exciting moment!

Steve was anxious to tell Mike and Delia what had happened but had to wait a while to share the good news because they, too, were praying with friends and loved ones touched by their story of life change. Their wedding became more than a celebration on the Gila River Indian Community; it became a party in heaven, welcoming prodigals home!

29

ARRESTED

DAN SCHAFER

"Trust in the LORD with all your heart and lean
not on your own understanding."
— Proverbs 3:5

I had been arrested!

Not in the usual sense. I had been arrested by words. Stan Toler, my best friend, and the coauthor of this book, had died after a year-plus battle with cancer. Every appearance was that he was going to beat it. But just two weeks before his death he took a sudden turn, and we all lost one of the greatest Christian leaders of our time.

The words of Stan's wife, Linda, arrested me.

At the funeral, she was undoubtedly whirling from the sudden change of circumstances. Nevertheless, she spoke with great composure. "Because I trust God's heart, I can submit to his will." I was captured by those words.

What a wonderful faith! What a testimony to the love of God!

Unfortunately, many Christians are more fair-weather followers than Linda. They turn back the moment that Jesus' words get hard (John 6:66) or give up when His will leads them into troubled waters.

This is particularly problematic given the fact that Jesus told us that in this world, we would have trouble. We cannot escape this reality. So, if we are only going to trust Him when all goes well, then we won't walk with Him long. But in this same announcement of Jesus about our troubles, we also have His words of comfort. Take heart. I have overcome the world.

Jesus has declared the outcome even before the troubles begin. Like Linda Toler, we only need to trust His heart. And when we do, we will be able to submit to His will.

THINK ABOUT THIS

"Because I trust God's heart, I can submit to his will."
– Linda Toler

MY PRAYER

Lord, help me to walk so close to you that I can trust Your heart, and therefore, be able to submit to Your will. Amen.

TRY IT

Ask 3 friends how they know they can trust the heart of God.

STORIES OF TRANSFORMATION

An Unprecedented Harvest

Dr. Dan Schafer/ President of WGM

The Call, *December 2017*

Shocking! Unfathomable! In every direction I looked, there were signs of significant deterioration. I was standing in the heart of Cairo, Egypt. This once thriving city now reeled under economic devastation. This devastation has arisen partly from the Arab Spring uprisings, partly from the loss of tourism purposefully orchestrated by Islamic terrorists, partly from the spiritual darkness that holds the majority of its citizens captive, and partly from the constant tensions among the various factions of Islam.

These economic challenges affect the very fabric of Egyptian society. They leave people struggling to make ends meet, communities suffering from high levels of unemployment, and a whole society questioning whether there is any real hope for the future.

Matthew 9:36 (NASB) captures a similar scene: "Seeing the people, He [Jesus] felt compassion for them, because they were distressed and dispirited like sheep without a shepherd." But Jesus saw more than just their mental and spiritual devastation; He also saw the openness to the gospel that their difficult circumstances had produced—a plentiful harvest.

As I stood there in Cairo, I realized that the men, women, and children I saw represented millions upon millions of Muslims who are living in distress across the Middle East and Northern Africa. Unable to find hope in their religion to survive these difficult days, they have lost their spirit; Satan has stolen it from them. That's the bad news. The good news is that this has made them a plentiful harvest field.

But before you rejoice, there is a challenge: "the workers are few" (Luke 10:2). In fact, many Christian workers have pulled out of these areas of the world because of the increased danger. The workers are decreasing at a time when the harvest is ripening. In fact, there are more Muslims—and not just a few more, exponentially more—coming to the saving knowledge of Jesus Christ right now than there have ever been in the history of Islam.

Several factors have brought about this unprecedented harvest, not the least of which is the people's disillusionment with Islam, partially brought about by militant groups like ISIS. Another attributing factor is that the governments of many Muslim majority countries are so occupied with bringing stability back to their countries that they are too busy to suppress the evangelistic efforts of Christians.

This opportunity will likely be short-lived, so we must act now before the door closes again! Jesus gave us the strategy we need for this abundant harvest. Pray to "the Lord of the harvest to send out workers into his harvest" (Luke 10:2 NET). At WGM, we've been praying; and God is, of course, answering those prayers. He is raising up workers for His harvest field. He also instructed us to act: "Go therefore and make disciples" (Matthew 28:19 NKJV).

ABOUT THE AUTHORS

DAN SCHAFER is an author, speaker, and missions leader who is president of World Gospel Mission, a global outreach organization with headquarters in Marion, Indiana. He served as a pastor for 12 years, and for the last 27 years has served as a missionary and missions leader. A graduate of Ohio Christian University, Dan has an MBA from Indiana Wesleyan University, and a Doctorate in Business Administration from Anderson University. He and his wife, Pam, reside in Marion, Indiana and have 2 children, Kevin and Julie, and 6 grandchildren. **www.wgm.org**

STAN TOLER Stan Toler was a dynamic speaker, leadership expert and best-selling author. He served for many years as vice president of John Maxwell's INJOY Leadership Institute, training church and corporate leaders to make a difference in the world. Prior to his untimely passing in 2017, he authored over 100 books with sales of more than 3 million copies. He was devoted to his wife, Linda, his sons, Seth and Adam, and 5 grandchildren who adored their "pookie." His legacy of timeless and enduring teachings is available at **www.stantoler.com**.